FIND YOUR PURPOSE
MASTER YOUR PATH

MATTHEW B. JAMES, MA, PHD

www.nlp.com

www.huna.com

FIND YOUR PURPOSE
MASTER YOUR PATH

MATTHEW B. JAMES, MA, PHD

ADVANCED NEURO DYNAMICS, INC.
75-6099 KUAKINI HIGHWAY HI KAILUA-KONA 96740

Find Your Purpose,
Master Your Path
1st Edition

PUBLISHED BY Advanced Neuro Dynamics, Inc.

75-6099 Kuakini Highway
Kailua-Kona, HI 96740

ISBN: 978-0-9845107-1-9

Printed in the United States of America

NLP.com

This book is dedicated to my wife Sumi, who has helped me in so many ways on my path. You have been a motivating force when I needed it, and a kick in the butt when necessary. You have made me want to be a better person, and this has helped me to dedicate to this path and excel beyond what I could have imagined. Thank you for loving, supporting and putting up with me over the years.

TABLE OF CONTENTS

FOREWORD

It's undeniable. We have entered into an unprecedented time of uncharted territories. Socially, politically, technologically, and psychologically, humankind has traveled far beyond the limits and imaginations of our ancestors. We face problems and puzzles no human has ever addressed, and our constantly expanding landscape of communication and information guarantees that the sands will continue to shift beneath our feet. Globally and personally, our decisions and choices have become weighted in a way that our great grandparents would not have understood.

We are so different from them, from each other. And yet we are connected by the tools and pathways our cultures, our planet and our own bodies have given us. These pathways, these tools, are both our solution and our challenge.

We live within a complicated dynamic, a profound moment, and a strange paradox. The evolution of our Selves and society now requires a transformative way of thinking we have not yet known. The change we create must be from a place that transcends the thinking that created our problems. It must move beyond our silent philosophies and intricately designed theories to become fully integrated into how we live and breathe.

New times require new approaches. But, if the new paradigm is not yet formed and even the way to think about it is not yet established, where do we begin? It seems an impossible riddle.

A challenging, yet poetic, irony is that we must be willing to turn our known world upside down – to release what seems real and embrace what feels uncertain. We must go up to go down; have less to have more; give to get; slow down to accomplish more. And we must give up the self we trust, to uncover the truth of who we are. We are being called to lose sight of the safe shores for a new and vibrant horizon that we cannot yet envision.

We can no longer seek the "right" path or teacher to tell us what to do or think. We find that we now crave the tools and frameworks to help us read the landscape. We require powerful and embracing paths to help us find our own answers. This is the gift that Dr. James has presented in this very special book.

Beyond wise philosophy – though there is plenty of wisdom in this book – you will find ancient and modern techniques converging to support the self-refining, self-redefining tools necessary to create a new experience of the world.

I have spent decades working with and learning from indigenous healers, and I know of few contemporary Western professionals who can walk the ancient paths of these healers and teachers while balancing the ancient tools with the best modern methods for healing and transformation. Matthew James has done this, through his thorough research and the lineage he has been chosen to carry.

It takes a fine character, a gifted mind and a profoundly open heart to navigate and merge the worlds of earth magic and spirit with the frontiers of neurology, psychology and day-to-day practicality. That is exactly what you will find in Find Your Purpose, Master Your Path.

Find Your Purpose, Master Your Path offers tools to deal with stress, relationships, and difficult choices within our complicated lives. It offers an incredible fusion of ancient and modern healing systems in a simple and straightforward way. These clear insights will enhance the understanding of advanced students and beginners alike.

But the most profound impact of Find Your Purpose, Master Your Path will come through your own commitment to the extraordinary opportunity before you. It is your choice, your commitment, your willingness, that will catalyze the lessons presented herein. As you read this special book, you will discover that magic is ordinary and the ordinary world is magical. You will come to understand that personal transformation is not only a gift you give to yourself. It will ultimately be your greatest gift to the world.

Jonathan H. Ellerby, Ph.D.
Akumal, Mexico, 2012

Featured as an expert in films, print, television, and radio, Jonathan Ellerby, Ph.D., is the author of "Return to the Sacred," "Your Spiritual Personality" and is the CEO of Tao Wellness Center and Inspired Living Community in the Riviera Maya of Mexico. Jonathan has over 20 years of experience in the fields of holistic healing, spiritual counseling, integrative medicine, and corporate consulting. Drawing from a PhD in comparative religion and travels to meet and study with healers and teachers in more than forty cultures around the world Jonathan makes spirituality simple and every day inspired. http://www.jonathanellerby.com

PREFACE

The term spiritual and spiritualty has taken on some new meanings in recent times. The words have been associated with so many different things. These associations are positive and negative, good and bad, happy and sad, and for many individuals, none of these labels apply. The problem is not with the label of spirituality itself, but rather the associations that so many have made.

I teach classes all around the planet and when I bring up the term spirituality, there are often murmurs in the audience – and with 150 to 200 people there in the room, murmurs do not go unnoticed.

I bring this up, because about six years ago now, I began to refer to our Huna Workshops as Consciousness Workshops. On our website huna. com, the event is called the Huna Higher Consciousness Workshop.

I did this because a while ago I realized that we were attracting non-spiritual people to the workshop. Now before you email me and explain that everyone is spiritual, let me agree: When you are on a spiritual path, you do see everyone as spiritual. However, depending on your particular path, you may not see it that way. That is to say, a person on a non-spiritual path may see everyone as being non-spiritual.

The realm of dichotomy or duality which so many of us live in, is one that must be transcended to experience the non-duality of concepts.

Let me simplify: Rather than debating a term like spirituality, religion or any other label, let's look at what we want to achieve as human beings is experiencing higher levels of consciousness. With this in mind, we quickly realize that each path is perfect, and each label we choose is perfect. If you want to be religious, GREAT! I am sure you want to be more conscious of your religious path, right? Likewise if you want to be more rational in life, being more conscious is vital, correct?

We live in amazing times in that energy is proven, personal empowerment is something we agree we could use more of, and increasing consciousness has become a part of our culture. This was not the case when I was teaching in the 90s, so I love our growth and expansion on the beautiful planet.

This book is about your consciousness and empowerment.

My five-year-old daughter asked me about energy after watching Avatar. She said, "Daddy, you teach about energy. How do I work with my energy?" Wow! What a great question! Not, "Daddy what is energy?" or worse, "That is just silly." She wanted to know what energy is and how she could apply it to her life.

Do you want to know what I said to her? "Skylar, do you know what lightning is?" She said "Yes!" I then explained that lightning comes down to earth in a flash. And that it usually looks for something to connect to that will ground it. I found a picture of a lightning rod, and explained that the energy then goes into the earth. She got it, oddly enough in a flash!

Then I said, "Skylar, your body is a lightning rod, and mana (Hawaiian for energy) comes from above, finds you, and connects / grounds in your body." She smiled and said, "How do I get more to come down!?!" I told her that is exactly what we have been teaching at our Huna workshop for 22 years now. "Wow, Daddy, that is a long time!!!"

Now, let's kick it up a notch for the adults. You are already connected to energy (read Dr. Lipton's book Biology of Belief or any Quantum Physics book). We are already on a path. Each path is different of course. However, there are similarities.

The similarities are that there are certain stages or doorways we have to pass through to achieve higher levels. From a Huna perspective, the big picture stages are called the lesson of mastery and the lesson of life. When I wrote this book a year ago, I realized that one way to approach higher levels of consciousness is through the path of individuation which Carl Jung taught. I also realized that Jung was much more "spiritual" than many thought during his lifetime, and that adding a Huna flare would help people absorb the concepts.

This book, and the next two that will follow, are meant to help the reader move from the realm of the ego driven society that we have created in Western thinking, to the realm of the true Self or Higher Consciousness.

Many students have said they avoid this type of study because they fear the loss of their identity. That is simply not the case with this type of work. Rather, think of moving from elementary school to middle school as my twelve-year-old son just did last year.

My son Ethan is the same person; he is just at a different level now. When you move through these doorways or stages, you are still you. Of course some things will change. Even so, a few friends that I have known for close to 20 years just said to me this year "Wow Matthew, you haven't changed at all! And yet you have...." They meant that I am the same person and yes, life has progressed, some doorways opened and I have passed through.

I hope this book, and the next two, help you on your path so that you may increase your consciousness and become more the "you" that you want to be.

Mahalo,

Matthew B. James, MA, PhD
DrMatt.com

Introduction

What's the Point?

If you picked up this book, you're most likely a seeker of some sort. You're on some kind of spiritual path or involved in human development. You've gone to workshops or read self-help books or tried different practices, all with the intention of becoming...what?

Papa Bray[1], a very wise Kumu Huna (teacher of Huna) who taught my father, said that we seek first the lesson of mastery then the lesson of life. The lesson of mastery is learning how to work with energy and bring it down to the physical to create your reality, for instance your health, relationships, money, needs and resources. The lesson of life means you take that foundation you created from the lesson of mastery and move back to spirit.

In modern psychology, the closest concept to the lessons of mastery and life comes from Carl Jung[2] and what he called the process of

---

1 David "Papa" Bray was the son of one of the last practicing Kahuna, David "Daddy" Bray. He instructed my father, Tad James, in the Bray family lineage of Huna.
2 Carl Jung, founder of Analytical psychology, was a prominent psychiatrist in the twentieth century who is best known for his work with dream analysis and

individuation, the process of becoming actualized or a truly authentic individual. Being authentic in this sense is more than being honest or even transparent. It means having all parts of yourself aligned to who you really are. Once you do that, you will find your purpose. And in the end, I'd say that this is what almost all of us are seeking: to feel fully aligned with who we are and our purpose.

Spiritual and human potential teachers often talk about the need to find your purpose though I've never found many books that clearly lay out how you do it. Each path is unique. Your path to finding your purpose will be different than your next door neighbor. But what all spiritual/ human potential paths have in common is some form of the lessons of mastery and life and, through them, connection with higher consciousness which is the source of your purpose. In fact, the focus of most of transpersonal psychology, much of the personal growth and development movement, Huna, and just about any esoteric study is to help us to find our purpose and to reclaim our true nature as fully authentic human beings.

But if this is our true nature, why do we have to "reclaim" ourselves as authentic human beings? Why do we have to chase it, study it, practice it and sometimes even struggle with it? Dr. Alex Docker, with whom I had the pleasure working with for a decade and who helped write the Jungian psychology section for Kona University's Master's Degree courses in Transpersonal Psychology, summed it up very simply: "We all think we're human beings, but we're actually a world of human doings."

---

symbolism. Areas of study that influenced his work include Eastern and Western philosophy, astrology, literature, alchemy, art and sociology.

I Can't Get No Satisfaction

Pay attention to what we call ourselves: human beings. Often we are so wrapped up in what we are doing that we forget or maybe never thought to stop and ask, "Who am I meant to be?" The words human being absolutely point to where our priority needs to be.

By the way, I don't even think we begin as human doings. We're human havings, as far as I'm concerned. Our focus has become: "If I just have this then I can be that." We live in a world that is materialistic – and that's how it is supposed to be. Personally, I own an iPhone and thank goodness I do! I have a computer. I have a car. I fully enjoy the physical world. The physical world is not evil, dirty or nasty, something to deny or make wrong. I'm not going to get deeply into what the physical world is or is not here. But I'd like to see us move away from focusing on the physical to reclaim the aspect that is called individuation, connection with higher self. Having more stuff doesn't make us more authentic or less authentic. But our relationship to stuff, the importance we give it, can lead us off the path.

Let me share what taught me the limitations of living my life as a human having: By 2002, I had worked for Advanced Neuro Dynamics, our training company, for ten years. My father took me out and bought me a Rolex. I was impressed and excited, thinking, "Wow. This means I finally made it!" As a teenager, I remembered my grandfather's gold watch that his company gave him for retirement. I played tennis in high school and, as a big tennis fan, saw Rolex splattered all over Wimbledon. So a Rolex was a big status symbol to me, very meaningful.

When my father gave me the Rolex, it had two interesting effects. First, I really treasured the watch as a marker on my personal path, and felt appreciation for the huge accomplishment of being with the organization for ten years and running it for five. Second, without taking anything away from that feeling of treasuring the gift itself, getting the Rolex did something else. It opened me up to a new realm and a very interesting way of thinking. I felt a visceral sense of accomplishment. I got a sense of "I have achieved something," and along with that came energetic euphoria. So every time I looked at my watch, I felt great!

Have you ever had that feeling, when you're looking at something that you just got that you weren't even sure you could ever get? Maybe it's a Lexus or a Rolex or your diploma or your first girlfriend/boyfriend or your first house – whatever that symbol of accomplishment was for you. Can you remember getting your first car? Every time you got behind the driver's wheel, remember that feeling? Especially in the beginning. "I did it! I have made it, man." Just seeing the symbol can bring back the great feeling, that high of "I have accomplished something and here is the physical, tangible proof."

But a few weeks or maybe a few years after acquiring that symbol (with my Rolex, it lasted a couple of months because it had a ruby in it!), someone asks, "What time is it?" and you say, "3:05." You look at your watch and that euphoric feeling isn't there anymore. "Oh, no! Did I get the wrong watch?" How many of you ever had that thought? Your internal system gets used to the experience and you don't feel it in the same way. But instead of understanding what truly happened, you freak out and think, "Oh, no. Was that the wrong car? The wrong watch? The wrong wife? Should I have gotten the other model? Maybe I should have gotten the solid gold. Or the blond." All of these thoughts start popping into your head. And instead of understanding what happened, what do most people do? Go shopping to get the next one and the next one and the next.

With my Rolex, I thought, "What happened? What happened to that feeling? What happened to the accomplishment? Where did it go?" I spent a short amount of time chasing after that feeling, but couldn't catch it. So I wondered, "If I can't get that feeling back, what does that mean? Did I not really accomplish what I had set out to accomplish? Did I miss it?" My questioning started off in a very innocent way questioning whether I got the wrong watch. But then it really snowballed.

Ringing the Bell of Being

Interestingly, this all happened at a time in my life where I was questioning who I should be and what I should really be doing with my life. When I asked that question out loud, my now brother-in-law said to me, "You shouldn't ask that, because once you ask it, you cannot un-ring that bell." And he was right. Once you ask the big questions of "why" or "what is the purpose", it's all over. Once you ask those questions, you can't un-ask them. To turn those questions off, you really have to go back to sleep. I'm not talking about head-on-the-pillow, snore and drool nighttime sleep. I'm talking about putting yourself back into the trance of the mundane, going through life as human havings and doings: wake up, shower, brush your teeth, get in the car, drive to work. To turn off those questions (which, trust me, is really hard) you have to become numb again. You have to shut off the part of your brain that craves to have purpose, that natural urge to have meaning in life.

So my experience with the Rolex snowballed into my asking, "If I'm not getting satisfaction from material stuff, if I'm not even sure why I'm doing what I'm doing, what's the point?" I started questioning everything: "Why am I doing what I'm doing? If I love Huna, why am I teaching NLP?" Then I'd question why I was even teaching Huna. All the questioning eventually pushed me into asking the real question: "Who am I really meant to be?"

The problem with not knowing your purpose is that you act and react but your actions don't feel good, and you just don't feel pono. Pono is that "Ah, this is right" feeling, and it only occurs when your actions are in alignment with conscious, unconscious, and higher self. My favorite explanation of pono is that feeling of unwavering congruency in your actions and being. When we're acting and reacting without that congruency and alignment, we usually get driven by the need to have or do the next thing: "I need to have a bigger house" or "I need to study under a different guru." Of course after a while, that next thing you have or do doesn't feel satisfying either.

Have you ever questioned what you're doing in your career, but instead of staying with the question, jumped to another job? Jumped from a rotten relationship to a different one? How did that work out for you? It's great in the beginning. But after a while, don't you wake up one day and realize you're still feeling the same lack of satisfaction?

Don't misunderstand me, there are times when you should get out of a job or relationship and the decision was great. I have met many people who really needed to change their situation or environment to get realigned. But too often we leave something only to re-create the same experience with another job or another person.

During my Rolex period, I decided to change my role within my organization. I thought I fixed the issue, only to find that I was still facing the exact same questions a short time later: "Why am I doing what I'm doing? Should I be doing something different?" And if you stay unaligned after you've started asking those critical questions, the lapse between doubting yourself seems to shorten. First you question what you are doing, make a change and a year goes by before you start questioning it again. But after the next change you make, the questioning begins at nine months. You make another change but you start questioning it after six months, until finally it's like you wake up questioning your actions and choices every single day. This is a sign that you're not yet on your path, following your purpose. Bottomline: Once being is your focus, you will find your purpose as well as your personal answer to "why am I doing this, having this, etc..."

OKAY, BUT HOW?

So I'm assuming that you've rung your own bell, that you've asked yourself those now-nagging questions that are stirring up your desire to know your purpose and to live it. I'm also guessing that, no matter where you are on your path, you've developed a substantial tool kit. Maybe you've learned to pray or access Higher Self through stillness. Maybe you've learned to breathe deeply to calm your emotions and clear your conscious brain. Maybe you've learned to make good decisions by laying out a list of pros and cons then sleeping on it. Maybe you have learned the benefit of running to reduce stress or counting to ten before speaking in anger. Maybe you've learned to interpret your dreams or listen to your intuition. All of this is useful. Yet even with all of these great tools, you may feel like you've been spinning your wheels. From my experience, in my own life and in working with my students, the real trick is to recognize where you are on your path and which tools to use at what times.

Let's take an example: Say, you come home from work and find that your very precocious toddler has experimented with using your DVD player as a toaster, shoving her peanut butter and jelly sandwich into it and waiting for it to pop out. You feel your internal volcano, your own active Kilauea, ready to erupt. What tool do you use? Maybe counting to ten is enough. Or maybe the incident triggers something deeper in you, like a traumatizing experience from your own childhood, and you need to do some work with your Shadow, that part of your subconscious that holds – and sometimes hides – negative aspects of yourself. Both are good tools, but you need to know where you are so you can use the right one. Needle-nose pliers are great but they aren't much help if the job calls for a sledge hammer!

Knowing where you are on the path is crucial for all students of spirituality, personal growth and development. If you don't know where you are on the path, if you have no idea of what you're doing, how do you know what the next step should be or what tool to use? How do you know if you should study quantum physics, energy work, hypnotherapy or astrology? Should you spend time to let go of more negative emotions or focus solely on connecting with your Higher Self? It would be like a football team not knowing where they are on the field. Should they kick a field goal, punt, throw the ball?? If you don't know where you are on the field, how do you know what to do!?

You can't really progress on your path until you know where you are on it. Here's an important truth that many people misunderstand: your path is not necessarily a linear, logical sequence of learnings. Too many people have the notion that "If I understand a certain level of consciousness, I'll never have to visit it again." Good luck with that! My students often tell me, "I've learned to flow energy and bring in Higher Self. So how come I still feel so much road rage on my way to work every morning?" They are assuming (wrongly) that they will no longer feel the frustrations of the ego or messages from the Shadow now that they have accessed higher states of consciousness.

The process is not as linear as it may sound. But if you've been a student of human potential or esoteric studies for quite a while and still feel inconsistent in your connection to higher self, you may not have fully integrated the Shadow yet. If you feel run ragged because of your expectations of yourself or others' expectations of you, you may not have made a clear distinction between persona and ego. In general, if you just don't feel pono or right with the world, some piece of self is probably hanging out there and needs to be brought in. Hawaiians call that "right with the world feeling" pono and, unlike many Westerners, they consider being pono a natural state – not just one for special occasions!.

In my experience, we don't work with a particular level of consciousness then transcend it to graduate to the next. (If you are sitting there thinking that you have progressed "beyond" the ego, I'm guessing you've got a few ego issues that could use some work!) Instead, the process of becoming authentic human beings and living our purpose is not "transcending" parts of ourselves but really about integrating all parts of ourselves: conscious, unconscious, and higher conscious.

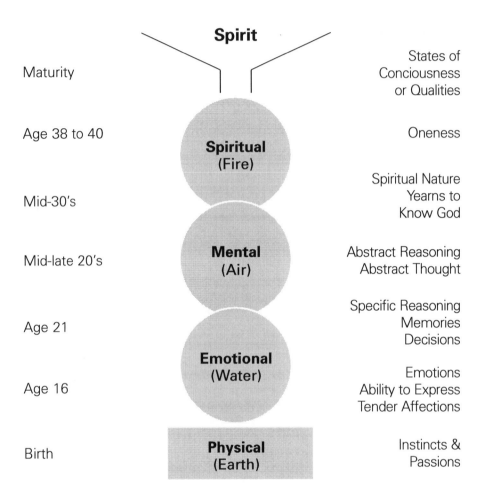

Maturity	**Spirit**	States of Conciousness or Qualities
Age 38 to 40	**Spiritual (Fire)**	Oneness
Mid-30's		Spiritual Nature Yearns to Know God
Mid-late 20's	**Mental (Air)**	Abstract Reasoning Abstract Thought
Age 21		Specific Reasoning Memories Decisions
Age 16	**Emotional (Water)**	Emotions Ability to Express Tender Affections
Birth	**Physical (Earth)**	Instincts & Passions

FOUR BODIES

So back to what most of us, at the end of the day, are really seeking: to live authentic lives, feeling fully aligned with who we are and connected to our purpose. Sometimes people think that it's going to be very difficult to figure out their purpose. Actually, it's not. It's very easy. This is what I want to share with you. I want to share how to find that purpose, how to connect with the path. It happens naturally through the process of individuation, understanding and integrating all aspects of ourselves.

Overview

There are straightforward steps to this process. Personally, though I've studied many others paths and disciplines, I've relied heavily on the teachings of Huna and the work of Carl Jung, both for my teaching and my own process. Jung and Huna share many similarities, and I've used their concepts and approaches throughout this book. The first step in the process of individuation is to understand – and accept – some basic concepts. In this book, I'll cover basic concepts, including a quick overview of the five major assumptions and the difference between the symbology and sign.

Then I'll delve into the major conscious mind work that needs to be done along the path including the roles that we play in life, which Jung referred to as persona, as well as the concept of ego and the role of ego. From Huna's perspective, ego and persona are simply your consciousness, but Jung made certain distinctions between the two that I think are helpful.

This book covers only the conscious mind, but it is important that you understand not only the defined role of the conscious mind, but also the unconscious mind and the Higher Self (which I will discuss in other books). That's the true lesson of life, knowing the role of each aspect of yourself and realizing that you wouldn't do anything without the involvement of all three aspects of who you are. We live in a society in which the ego or the persona, depending on what context you're talking about, drives everything else. In actuality, Jung, Papa Bray and anyone else who teaches anything spiritual or esoteric will tell you that's totally opposite to how it should be. Everything should flow from the Self (that is self with a capital "S"). And when all aspects of ourselves are integrated, when we experience ourselves as fully authentic human beings, this is naturally how it works.

So let's start by looking more closely at what Jung's concept of individuation and Huna's concept of life mastery really mean.

(!) SELF EXPLORATION:

To help you get the most out of this book, I've offered some questions and exercises throughout to help you apply the teaching. You might start a journal or simply contemplate the questions in your meditation time. Try not to judge yourself for your any of your answers. Just answer as truthfully as you can.

1. What tools do you have in your personal tool bag? How have they served you? What do you feel you are missing?

2. Can you recall a time when the "bell of truth" rang for you? Where has that taken you? Did you ever try to avoid its call? How did that work out for you?

INDIVIDUATION AND MASTERY

JUNG AND HUNA

As I mentioned, a lot of this series is based on the work of Carl Jung and the teachings of Huna as taught by my father's kumu (teacher), Papa Bray. On the surface, Carl Jung and Papa Bray have little in common. Jung was a renowned, cutting edge psychiatrist and founder of Analytical Psychology in the twentieth century. Papa Bray was the son of one of last practicing kahuna in the ancient tradition of Ho`omana[1]. But when you understand a little bit about these two individuals, it might make sense that I reference them so much.

For the most part, Carl Jung[2] stayed on the secular side of psychology. But he had periods when he was very involved in the esoteric. Actually, some of the works that he held back from publication until after his

---

1 Ho'omana is one of the original names for what is now commonly called Huna. It means empowerment or to empower.
2 Now, I really want to be clear: Through this book, even if I use the word Jungian, I'm basically referring to what Jung himself thought. To my mind, there are a lot of people who are Jungian who have taken his teachings down a path that I don't think Jung would have recognized.

death reveal that he was more spiritual and esoteric than his original writings showed him to be. Based on his day and culture, I think he made a conscious decision to stick to the scientific / psychological route. He may have thought that he could impact more people by taking this Western approach.

For example, in most of his work, Jung uses the term Self with a capital S. I think Jung used the Self with a capital S to avoid sounding too spiritual or religious. But in Memoirs, Dreams and Reflections, Jung explained that the Self can be religious, can be God. When Jung talked about the Self, it was all about what is inside of us. Anyone who has studied Jung and looked at his published work, especially after his death, can see that Jung thought that the concept of Self was anything that you want it to be. Jung said that the Self, with a capital S, is your god within. To Jung, individuation could mean simply psychological well-being or it could mean connection to God. Instead of using the word Self, you could use God, Goddess, higher consciousness, Higher Self.

Jung goes on record clearly accepting religious, spiritual, and occultist views. And he routinely looked at a patient's astrological charts and consult the tarot – not as you would for divination, but as you would for understanding archetypes, which Jung was well known for studying. Jung studied the kabala and had a deep understanding of esoteric studies. Jung didn't have a problem looking at dreams in a slightly different way than Freud or others in his generation did, or talking about things like the Shadow. But that said, Jung approached his work as a psychiatrist, not as a mystic.

Papa Bray took a very different route. Though he lived in the twentieth century, he chose to follow a path that was centuries old. Papa Bray's perspective was totally spiritual, esoteric and he didn't pay much attention to the science of modern psychology. He didn't question of the definition of Higher Self. From Papa Bray's perspective, the Higher Self was your own god or connection to God. It was your personal experience of the higher realms, the god within.

But though they approached it from different directions, Jung and Papa Bray came to many of the same conclusions. They both recognized a tiered approach to human consciousness that includes subconscious, conscious and higher conscious. They both felt that these three needed to be integrated. They both worked with dreams and with symbology that is personal as well as collective. To Jung, the goal for us as human beings is individuation. To Papa Bray and in Huna, the point of existence is mastery. (Both individuation and mastery are described further in the next section.)

You don't need to paint this as a religious path, a spiritual path, or a psychological path. It's a path. You can approach it psychologically. You can approach it religiously. You can approach it spiritually. You find people who are self-actualized in all three of these contexts, and any other context you can think of.

It's irrelevant as to how you label this spiritual, this Higher Self. Use your own personal label. Any time I use a label that doesn't fit in your model of the world, just translate it in your own mind. So if I mention Self, and you prefer the Hawaiian word, aumakua (which means guardian spirit and the word Papa Bray used to refer to Higher Self), think aumakua. Or think God or "the real me" or The Grinch Who Stole Christmas for that matter! The point is to find out what this connection that you're seeking is all about, no matter what you want to call it.

INDIVIDUATION

According to Jung, individuation is a process of psychological integration. The idea of individuation is to incorporate both the collective and personal subconscious into the conscious. In his writing Psychological Types, Jung described individuation as "the process by which individual beings are formed and differentiated [from other human beings]; in particular, it is the development of the psychological individual as a being distinct from the general, collective psychology." That may sound pretty complicated and esoteric, but it's not. It just means that all parts of your self are aligned, that all of your cylinders are firing, that you are totally comfortable in your own skin. Jung believed that individuation, or self-actualization as some call it, was the path to mental, emotional and physical well-being as well as the foundation for higher values like freedom, justice and universal harmony.

HUNA'S LESSONS

According to Huna, as taught by Papa Bray, the point of existence is to experience the lesson of mastery and the lesson of life. Mastery means learning how to take universal energy, bring it down to become pono with the physical realm. The lesson of life is to rise up from that foundation and move back to Spirit. The areas most related to the lesson of mastery are relationships, the work you do, financial wellbeing, and health and fitness. The areas most related to the lesson of life (taking the energy back up to spirit) are spirituality, and personal growth and development.

What I mean by "areas most related" is that your foundation (bringing the energy down in the lesson of mastery) is created by becoming pono – that sense of feeling right with yourself and the world – in your paths related to career, health and fitness, and relationship. When you are pono in these areas, it is as if you have a solid foundation and are able to pursue a spiritual path with that solid backing. This is in no way to imply that you need to be in a single-partner relationship or that you need to have a strong sense of career in the normal sense or that you have to be buff and toned. In fact, some of the most spiritual people I have known were not in relationships. Others did have what we'd recognize as a specific career focus and some definitely did not meet Western standards of being physically fit. But these people were totally pono with their path of being alone, doing whatever occupation they happened to be doing and, in some form, in tune with their bodies.

IS IT POSSIBLE?

Sometimes, the idea of mastery, connection to Spirit, individuation or self-actualization feels too mysterious, esoteric, far away, unattainable. For most people, the daily norm is to feel unstable, unsure, uncertain, pretty much at the mercy of whatever is happening around and to them. To many people, this is just how it's supposed to be.

But have you ever had a moment where you were just in the flow, where you knew you were connected with higher consciousness, and information was just flowing through you? Where it all felt effortless, and nothing could have shaken you off of your foundation? That's what it feels like to be connected to Spirit or, as in Jung's process of individuation, to be self-actualized and experience your authentic self.

Abraham Maslow was an American psychologist who focused on the process toward individuation or actualization as well. He studied a number of exceptional individuals such as Abraham Lincoln. Maslow found that, despite all of his many failures in life – and Lincoln had more than his share – Lincoln had the ability, even with everything falling apart around him, to be fully confident. Someone on Lincoln's staff would say, "Are you sure?" and he could respond, "Yep, This is the way we're doing it. I know who I am. I know what we're doing. This is the path. This is the way we're moving forward."

The Dalai Lama is another example of a person who has, in my humble opinion, achieved the level of individuation. In addition to what he has endured personally and as a part of a displaced group of people, he teaches and lectures in a way that demonstrates the qualities Maslow talked about. My Kumu Etua Lopes had the honor of meeting him and hosting him here on the island of Hawai`i, and apparently, at the end of many of his talks, the Dalai Lama says something along the lines of, "Now that is what I have to share, and you may take it or leave it. Do what you want with the information." Now I am sure that it is much more elegant than that but this is from a guy who's been honored with tons of awards, including the Nobel Peace Prize, for his work on interfaith harmony, peace and the environment. And still, people who have met and listened to him say that he shares freely, without ego, and is always quietly confident in his approach. I read a quote from him: "I find hope in the darkest of days, and focus in the brightest. I do not judge the universe." Definitely someone who is secure in his foundation.

Building Your Foundation

Of course, it's not only Presidents of the United States or international spiritual leaders who have this foundation. But both Lincoln and the Dalai Lama obviously reflect an unshakeable foundation and are what Maslow called "self-actualized." It's the same feeling you have when you have connection to Higher Self and I think we've all had this experience at some time or another. But since we've all had the experience of that unshakeable foundation, why is it so important to go back and deal with persona, ego, shadow, etc.? Why can't we just focus on staying in that state?

Bottom line? For that unshakeable foundation to be consistent, you have to do the work on all levels of yourself. I know because I've been there. I'd be connected to my Higher Self and I would have moments on stage while teaching, or in my life in general when it would be flowing. But then I stopped or it stopped. You know why? Because there were certain things I didn't take care of along the way.

At this stage of the game, when I'm not on foundation I say to myself, "Man, this is a weird feeling, to be unstable." My normal experience has become: "I'm on foundation, connected." Was it always like this for me? Definitely not! I was up and down and all around, despite the fact that I was sincerely working my path. But like all of us, I'd be on the path, have a connection with higher self then have to stop and start with persona all over again. It was really irritating! But I realized that you can't just gripe about it or avoid it. If the work is not complete on some level, it's not complete. But trust me: if someone like me can do the work it takes to reach the point where foundation feels like the norm, you can too.

And here's the important point: this is not good or bad, happy or sad – it just is. Many teachers will explain that these issues or situations that you bump into are really the curriculum that you need on your journey. It's like math: you might jump into calculus without having algebra down pat. But at a certain point, if you may need a refresher course in algebra to move forward. No big deal. It's not good or bad, just necessary.

And honestly, the work is not that much when you think about what you gain. Just re-imagine those moments when you felt totally connected, when you were just in the flow, when you felt that unshakeable foundation. Now what would it be like if that was your normal experience throughout the day? Even if you experienced that feeling twice a day, just day and night, wouldn't that be good? Wouldn't it be great to feel that this sense of connectedness is just the way life is? Rather than having "peak experiences" on rare occasions, to feel that stability, certainty, foundation and flow as the norm?

One of my trainers, Nicholas, was a particularly sharp kid. Not only was he smart (in college by age 15!), Nicholas was also very spiritually aware at a young age. But in the social arena, Nicholas just didn't have it. He felt painfully self-conscious around others, always second-guessing what he said or did. Like all of us, he learned to hide it, to appear cool and collected though he didn't feel it.

At 18, Nicholas was deeply wounded when a long-time girlfriend broke up with him. He hid out for a while and dove into his spiritual books. One book about healing said something like "the deepest healing only comes from connection with Higher Self." It hit Nicholas like a ton of bricks and he started sobbing uncontrollably. "The closest I can explain it is that I felt the presence of his Higher Self. And I felt like I was 'me' for the first time ever." Through this experience, Nicholas finally began to feel pono, totally aligned with who he truly was – and with that sense of his true self, his social awkwardness and anxiety disappeared. Nicholas still had some work to do, so he set about consciously identifying and addressing his negative self-image. Years later when a client with similar social anxiety described his symptoms and stress, Nicholas could only barely remember that he had once lived with that same pain.

Could Nicholas have just continued as he was, feeling anxious in social situations yet hiding it? Sure. But by doing the work necessary, Nicholas now feels pono most of the time. It not only shows in his own life but in the contribution he makes to others.

THE HAPPINESS FACTOR

One more big picture, abstract, or chunked-up way of looking at individuation and the lessons of mastery and life: It's really about learning how to find happiness. Happiness doesn't come from having the things. It doesn't come from doing what you're doing. Happiness comes from being the person that you are meant to be. That's where true happiness comes from. When I look at anything that we do in life, I have found that it boils down to happiness, wanting to wake up and just be happy with yourself. When you are happy with yourself, you're happy with the rest of the world. When you are happy with yourself, when you are being the person that you're meant to be and you're living your purpose, what you are meant to do flows from that.

No Earthquake Necessary

The other thing that I think is really important to state is that when I discovered who I was meant to be, it didn't create any upheaval in my life. It didn't create any upheaval in my relationship. It didn't create any upheaval in what I do. It transformed what I do and allowed me to shed roles I used to play in the organization that don't fit with who I am. But I didn't get a job change by discovering who I am. Oddly enough, you may find that you're already in a job that is what you're meant to do or the relationship you're meant to have.

Sometimes people think, "If I discover my ultimate purpose and become self-actualized, I might go live in a cave." No, that's not the aim of this either. Caves are highly overrated. How many of you have heard the old song I Want to Go Back to My Little Grass Shack? But Uncle George Na'ope[3] used to say, "Well, I don't want to go back to my little grass shack. I like my running water. I like my indoor toilet. I like my microwave oven, and especially my TV!"

---

3 Uncle George Na'ope was one of my beloved teachers and an expert in chants and hula. He has been named by the State of Hawai'i as a Golden Living Treasure and is the founder of the Merrie Monarch Hula Festival.

The idea here is to find happiness, to become pono so that you know who you are, and often that happens within the life you've already created. You just add to your life that you know who you're meant to be. What you do flows from that. Then what you're meant to have actually comes to you. You don't have to go out there and hunt it down, or spend your whole life chasing after some great white whale.

THE SEED YOU PLANT

Within this process of self-actualization, we have to take ownership of what we experience on our path. The idea that "we create our experience" is becoming almost mainstream these days. But what does it really mean?

Etua[4], one of my teachers in Huna, says that every day you're given an ano`ai (a seed) and the goal is to plant that seed. When you plant that seed, it grows and bears fruit. The problem is that most people in our society haphazardly plant things then complain that they aren't getting what they wanted. My wife, Soomi, had a grandmother who used an interesting saying from Korea. The rough translation is, "If you plant sprouts, you get sprouts. And if you plant apples, you get apples." Too many people spend their lives complaining after they planted sprouts that there are no apples growing! Soomi's grandmother said, "Life is really simple. If you want apples, plant apples."

There's a huge lesson there. A lot of us love that idea of self-actualization, of having energy, waking up feeling absolutely magnificent and wanting

---

4 Etua Lopes has been one of my primary teachers for many years; and he was a prominent student of the late George Na'ope. Etua is the honored hula instructor at Hulihe'e Palace.

to tackle the day. But some of us still go out and party and drink, blowing out all our energy. We wake up feeling rotten the next day and wonder why. If you plant that seed, guess what you get? This applies to every area of your life. If every time you walk into your job and say, "What a stupid job," what are you planting? What do you expect to get back? Because if you plant something negative, that's what you get.

What we need to do is take back control. In life, you don't just reap what you sow. You get to enjoy the harvest of what you've put out there. That whole saying, "you reap what you sow," literally means that you're going to have to deal with whatever it is that you plant on the path. Papa Bray referred to it as the law of karma or the law of cycles and rhythms. The energy that you plant comes back to you. You grow what you sow.

THE HAND YOU'RE DEALT

I shared this concept with one student, and his response was interesting. He said, "Yeah, but I've been dealt an awful hand." In almost every single lineage, in every single system that I've studied, the kumu, guru or teacher, would have a similar response: "In actuality, you weren't dealt the hand. You picked the hand, down to every single card, number and suit. And this life is about figuring out why you gave yourself this hand." If you ever think, "I was dealt a bad hand," go look in the mirror. You're looking at the dealer.

Most of us know the hand that we were dealt. The why you dealt yourself that hand is your purpose. The why is the answer. The why comes when you have that connection with Higher Self. But rather than focusing on discovering that why, we tend to sit around and complain about the hand. Yet when you answer why you gave yourself this hand, things tend to flow pretty effortlessly. Having that answer definitely gives you a level of ability to plant what you want on your path, to watch it grow, and to enjoy the harvest of what you have planted.

Happiness is an empowering moment when you clearly realize that you dealt yourself the hand you hold and you can look at your hand and understand why. It's an amazing experience when you wake up, as I did, one morning and could see from my earliest memory to where I am now how every piece fits. From why I created my specific parents to why I'm Caucasian to why I live in Kailua Kona to why I spent two years working in a photography studio learning to put makeup on women!

Even that odd piece fell into place. How? I am often a guest on TV now, and it's rare that they provide someone to do make up for guests. If you appear on TV without make up, as Nixon painfully realized when he debated JFK, you're not going to look that great. But because of my stint in the photography studio, I do a better job than some of the makeup artists studios hire. I know how that piece fits, and I cannot begin to describe how good that feels when every piece of the puzzle that you've lived up until now just fits.

By the way, the good and the bad, the happy and the sad, the beautiful and the ugly – it all fits. When you see that and come to realize how amazing certain points along that path have been. At one point, I thought my life was just a coin toss, 50/50. "Matt, we're going to make you an assistant manager of Harpo's Pizza. There are two stores. You can either go to Windward Mall, or you can go to Pearl City." I literally flipped a coin, went to Pearl City and ended up meeting the person who introduced me to Soomi, my wife. If I'd gone to Windward Mall, I would never have met him so I never would have met her. Yet life can seem like a bundle of arbitrary choices: "What the heck, I'll turn left. Who knows why?"

But when you find your purpose, all of these arbitrary choices and moves just fit into place. And when they do and you can see it, life's easier. The path no longer feels like it's uphill. The path no longer feels like you don't know what's coming around the next turn. It's as if the path flattens out, or like someone just tossed you a map so you know where the turns are coming. Life becomes like a crop you've planted: you know why you planted apples and when you planted them so you know that the fruit of this planting is just around the corner. It's almost irrelevant what you planted; you can enjoy it because you know you planted it and that it's part of your path and purpose.

ⓘ SELF EXPLORATION

1. How would you describe the connection you are seeking? How will you feel when you feel this connection?

2. How pono do you feel in your life? Is it different in different areas of your life? If so, which areas would you most like to improve? Does that feeling of pono seem to change with season or circumstance? If so, how and when?

3. Think of a time you felt in the Zone or in the flow. What qualities did you feel?

4. Are there people in your life that you consider self-actualized and/ or mature individuals? What qualities do they have? How do you feel around them? (If you can't think of anyone in your life with this strong foundation, think of people you might know about, historical figures or even fictional characters.)

5. How do you define happy and/or happiness?

6. What seeds have you planted in your life? How intentional or unintentional were these seeds? How do you feel about the results?

7. Think about the hand you've been dealt. Can you see yet how the cards fit for you? Are some still a mystery? Why might you have chosen those particular cards?

1: Perception
is Projection

5: Law of
Attraction

2: Cause
and Effect

4: Cycles and
Rhythms

3: Creation

Five Basic Assumptions

The five basic assumptions are critical for anyone following a spiritual path. An assumption is a foundational idea, the basis from which you view everything else. Without understanding and accepting these five assumptions, it's pretty impossible to move forward on the path to self-actualization and connection to Higher Self. These basic truths show up in different forms in most spiritual or human potential systems. In this series, I'll be presenting them as I learned them from Huna. At Huna, we actually focus on four basic assumptions then I throw in the law of attraction as a fifth. Papa Bray taught that you need to incorporate these five basic assumptions in everything you do.

1: Perception is Projection

The first of the four basics is perception is projection. Perception is projection says that you're not so much perceiving the external world as you are projecting what you carry inside out onto the world around you. So the world is a reflection of your inner thoughts, feelings, values, beliefs. In other words, the outer world is a reflection of what's going on inside.

People tend to take two extreme views on this basic assumption. Some people reject it completely. "That's not possible. There is a table here. It's not just in my head." They take a very physical, Newtonian, point of view. Others go to the opposite extreme, especially when they first learn this concept. "Everything is inside my head. You don't even exist. You're not real. Therefore, I can treat you however I want." I remember in the early days of Neuro-Linguistic Programming (NLP), if someone said something nasty to someone else, the speaker would justify it with, "Well, perception is projection." Even as a 13-year-old, I couldn't buy that life worked that way.

Perception is projection is not an absolute but exists along a spectrum. Jung, of all people, would have recognized this and would have applauded Huna's perspective on this. For example, I think Jung would have hated the way that individuals walk around today and proclaim, "I'm an extrovert." No, you're not. You're more than just an extrovert, and if you weren't more than just an extrovert, your life would be completely messed up. You're extroverted or introverted contextually along a spectrum. For example, in the context of hanging out on the beach with your best buddies, you might feel – and act – like a full-blown extrovert. But in the context of meeting your prospective in-laws for the first time, you might feel and act more like an introvert. In Science and Sanity, Alfred Korzybski[1] proposed the idea of doing away with all labels because we tend to use a label to lock ourselves in a box in our society.

1 Albert Korzybski was a twentieth century philosopher and scientist. His research concluded that we do not perceive reality directly but only through our particular cultural beliefs. One of his most famous sayings was: "The map is not the territory."

But we are not in a box; all aspects of personality are contextual along a spectrum.

What about dualities? Isn't it either day or night, dark or light? No, it's not. Though we tend to lock into these dualities as if they are absolute, just live in Alaska for a while. Day is very different and night is very different at certain times of year. Here in the islands, day and night is different. Whether you live in Kailua Kona or in Hilo, day and night can be different. So day and night are not absolute fixed points.

Another example would be masculine and feminine. A century ago, most cultures had pretty strict definitions of what was "manly" or "womanly" and you were a complete misfit if you exhibited feminine characteristics as a man or masculine characteristics as a female. Today, most of us are more comfortable that, no matter what our gender, all of us are both masculine and feminine. We all have a soft side. We all have a tough side. Each of us runs along the feminine/masculine spectrum, and we change where we are on that spectrum depending on context. Women might find themselves being a little more "masculine" in work situations. Men might show their "feminine" side when they are with small children.

So most things are not purely objective, black or white. And this applies to perception is projection as well. Take the example of the floor beneath your feet: You're in a room with a floor. Based on the 126 bits[2]

---

2 *Mihaly Csikszentmihalyi is a leading researcher in the psychology of happiness. In his book Flow, he notes that our brains process 126 bits of information in every moment, rejecting or ignoring millions of other bits of information presented to us in the same moment.*

of information you are picking up at this moment, you know there is a floor. Anyone walking into that room would collectively acknowledge that there is a physical solid floor in the room. That's not in your head. You can't change the reality of it – unless you bring in a bulldozer and some dynamite. But short of demolition, this floor is going to remain beneath you.

In a sense, you have less control over the experience of the floor than other experiences. Yet you still have some control over the experience because there's a certain portion of your experience of that floor that is entirely in your head. Do you like it? Do you like the color? Do you hate the color? Do you wish it were cleaner? Did you even notice it? Do you even care? All of that is completely in your head, your projection.

When students or teachers polarize the "perception is projection" issue by saying that either everything is in your head or it's all external reality, they miss the point. Of course, there's a floor, whether you like it or not, whether it's even in your awareness, whether there is any emotional hook or not. The floor exists, period. But there is a certain percentage of control on any part of the spectrum that you always have, and it is your reaction to that experience. You always have one-hundred-percent control over your reaction.

MEDICINE, PSYCHOLOGY AND PERCEPTION IS PROJECTION

Over two decades ago, a research project reported in the Journal of the American Medical Association stated that anger is bad for the heart. This may not seem surprising to many of us. Yet I still run into people who say, "I am not really sure if the mind affects the body that much. I want to be healthy, so why am I sick?" Others say things like, "I don't believe in those medical doctors. They don't know anything about the mind-body connection." I'm sorry but they knew this before most of us did. Within medicine, it's beyond understood that there is a level of your perception that affects your physical reality, all the way down to your physical wellbeing. I've also seen many studies that say that your beliefs, your thinking have to be on board with any treatment (whether physical, psychological, energetic, or spiritual) that you undertake. If you do not believe and are not fully invested and dedicated to a treatment, the chances of the treatment working have been proven to be far less. That's perception is projection.

When it comes to something like an emotion, that's an experience that is entirely internal and within your control, though you may not always feel like you have that control! Psychology and medicine have had trouble helping people control their emotions because they're attempting to fix emotional issues with methods that don't necessarily get to the source of the issues. These methods (i.e. various psychotherapies or psychopharmaceuticals) do work for some people. But the truth is that we know more about the dark side of the moon than we do our mind and how it works. People seemingly have similar emotional problems and some experts argue they understand these problems. But what helps one person doesn't necessarily help another. We have yet to find the magic pill that will fix all problems. That's why it's important to understand yourself and how the aspects of yourself function. Like a diet, not every mental and emotional approach to wellbeing is going to work for everyone. But by understanding yourself, you'll know what tools to use.

1. Spend a day loosening up your point of view. Throughout your day, use this question frequently: How might I see this situation/person/ issue differently? (Another powerful question, especially if you feel stuck about something or someone: What if I'm just totally wrong about my perception of this!)

2. Look around at your current surroundings. Putting your focus on one thing at a time, pause and pay attention to underlying thoughts or feelings that might color the reality of that thing. For example: "That's the mirror my mother gave me. She was beautiful and it's beautiful." Or "I don't like that sweater. My ex gave it to me. It looks cheap."

2: CAUSE AND EFFECT

The second basic assumption is cause and effect. We're all pretty comfortable with a cause and effect universe, right? When we see something happen or see a particular result, we assume that something or someone caused it, even if we can't see that someone or something. But this basic assumption takes the dynamic of cause and effect a little further: If something in your life happens or you get a certain result, on some level you are the cause of it. Your life doesn't happen to you, it happens through you. Cause and effect says for every act, there is a reaction. That's basic physics. Realize that you are the creator. Realize that you are the creator of your experiences. And if you want a different result, you are the one who can – and must – cause it to be different. For many people, this is a radical way to see the world and their lives. On the one hand, it's a great freedom to know that you really are in control, that you really are the cause – not the victim – of events in your life. At the same time, it can feel like a lot of responsibility. For some people, overwhelming and confusing: "How could I have possibly caused that?!?"

Yep, with cause and effect, you really need to grasp that, at the end of the day, there's just you. You are responsible for getting your results. That doesn't negate asking for support, taking a training, maybe getting someone to guide you. When you visit a medical doctor, you expect to get a certain level of treatment and help for whatever's bothering you. If you go to an attorney, you expect to get a certain level of service and assistance with your legal issues. Some people might argue, "Then I'm not responsible in that situation. The medical doctor (or lawyer or expert) is supposed to steer me." Getting assistance is one thing. But giving all of your power away and claiming you have no control over it whatsoever, that's just not the truth of how things work.

Papa Bray said that, on a certain level, you are 100 percent responsible for the results that you get. You are the cause. This means you can't go to a workshop, a lawyer, or a doctor, then blame these experts if you don't get the results you wanted. But that's a pretty common attitude in today's world, isn't it? "I didn't get the results that I wanted. Whose fault is it? Let's get some money from them!" That's an unfortunate position to take because it perpetuates being at effect rather than being at cause.

Are there instances where someone is truly deserving of a settlement, or something happens that really shouldn't have happened? Sure. But Papa Bray would say that even in those situations, at some level, you created the experience for a reason. The question isn't about fault or blame. If it was up to me, fault and blame are words that I'd eradicate. It has nothing to do with fault or blame. It has to do with responsibility. Why did you create this event? And, here is the key: what is the learning that you need to get from it? Because once the event is over, as the old saying goes, "No use crying over spilt milk." You have to learn from that experience – or spend a lifetime mopping up wet floors!

One of my students is a beautiful woman who became a model at age 15 and an actress in her 20's. From early on, she went through a number of bad relationships with men, even a sexual assault and a marriage that included abuse and infidelity. Though she had an innate sense that she was "responsible" for these experiences, it was more from a sense of being guilty or "to blame" for them. "I knew that I was somehow attracting this bad stuff to me. But I thought it was because there was something wrong with me." She went through some really dark times of bulimia and even self-cutting. After attending one of our workshops and understanding what cause and effect really means, she's been able to break many of the patterns. "Now I understand that these experiences have learnings attached to them. I have the power to find the learnings, to change my response to a situation and to choose what situations I get into." Though she tells me that she hasn't yet found "the one," she now has much more positive relationships with the men in her life.

I love that old joke that goes: "Doctor, every time I do this, it hurts." And the doctor says, "Well, stop doing that, then." At some level, you've got to come to the conclusion that, "Okay. If I keep bumping my head up against this wall, the wall's not going to come down. In a battle between my skull and that wall, it looks like the wall will win every time." Stop doing that then! You are the cause of your headaches, not the wall! Doing the same thing over and over again, thinking you'll get a different response, is defined as insanity.

But if we don't like something, the kneejerk reflex in our society is to blame something or someone else. "My life is ruined because my parents weren't attentive." "I'm not doing well at work because my boss is a jerk." Rather than taking responsibility, we position ourselves as victims, the effects of someone or something else. We've set ourselves up as powerless.

One of my favorite examples of this: I teach in a rural area in Canada and the hotel's training room is pretty rustic. One of the participants took it upon herself to go home and bring me a rug and a few fake plants for the funky stage. Very nice gesture and it warmed my heart. We got rolling on the session and, within the first half hour, some guy in the front raised his hand and said: "Is there anything you can do about the stage, because I'm getting no value out of this training because your stage is so ugly." This guy had given his entire experience away to a rug and a few fake plants!

That example may seem extreme, but I've seen people blame the most obscure and insignificant things to avoid getting any results whatsoever out of a workshop, to make sure that they have no responsibility for their experience.

REWARDS FOR BEING AT EFFECT

We live in a society that actually rewards being at effect in some contexts more than being at cause. When you are rewarded for being at effect, you perpetuate it. "Who do we blame? How can we get some money from them? And how do I make sure I maintain that state of being at effect? Because if I become cause and am responsible for my life, I will lose all the benefits of being at effect." For example, someone may stay in an abusive relationship feeling victimized because she gets sympathy from friends because of it, or maybe even an invitation to be on Jerry Springer ! This is what's called secondary gain. Psychology talks about secondary gain a lot these days because people receive benefit from having a problem that outweighs getting rid of the problem. So they're better off keeping their problems, and it's easier to keep your problems if you don't claim any responsibility for them.

THE POWER OF CAUSE

Cause and effect is not an easy assumption to live but it is one that is truly empowering. It's important in this context because we're talking about your path. It's not my path. I've got my path and I don't need your path. And you don't want my path. You want your path. You have to be 100 percent responsible for moving down your path. That's it. If your path is uphill, you've got to find a way to get over that hill. If it's downhill, you got to find a way to make sure you slow down enough so that you don't crash and burn.

What if you do crash and burn? What if you fall on your path? I like the way Patanjali in the Yoga Sutra's expressed it. He said that to curse the very act of falling down on the path may be to curse the very thing you needed to move to the next level. It's counterproductive to beat yourself up for the down times, because that may be the thing that gets you up. You've got to get up, dust yourself off, and take responsibility but not blame. That's important so let me repeat it: take responsibility, not blame. Cause and effect is not a complex existential inquiry into finding a reason why for everything. No. It's a very simple and easy concept. It basically says that, at the end of the day, there's only you looking back in the mirror.

I've NEVER heard anyone say, "I'm at the end of my life and I did everything my heart desired. If my gut said to go do it, I'd do it. I've been there. I've done that. I've experienced more love than I wanted. What a bummer. Man, I wish I had never lived so fully." Nope, I've NEVER heard anyone say that. What I do hear when I meet people who haven't done everything they've wanted to do: "I wish, I should have, I could have, I would have." Cause and effect says get rid of the shoulda, coulda, wouldas, and just do it. We're talking about becoming the person you want to be. Once you know who you want to be, you do have to just do it.

(!) SELF WORK:

1. For a moment, feel the difference between accepting responsibility for something versus feeling that you are "to blame" for something. Which feeling makes you feel more energized to take action?

2. Think about situations where you felt you were the victim. Can you imagine how you might have been the cause of those situations? Is it possible those situations were there to teach you something? If so, what might that be?

3. Think about situations where you feel that you have no control. Maybe it's the economy, the behavior of your boss, the weather. Where is your power in that situation?

3: CREATION

The next basic assumption flows almost directly from cause and effect. It is creation. The assumption of creation says is that, in order for something to come into existence, the opposite also has to come into existence. That our world, that all of existence is a part of a duality or dichotomy, day and night, light and dark, happy and sad. Some people might use "happy and happier" as the dichotomy. Another person would think of "happy and sad." With things that are internal, Papa Bray said that you had total, not just partial, but total control over the experience of the dichotomy. So if you create happy and sad as the dichotomy, Jung would say that you are doomed to move back and forth between happiness and sadness. Even existence is part of a dichotomy: you either exist, or you don't exist.

What does that mean? Well, if there are either good or bad relationships in your universe, or if, according to your belief, all relationships have highs and lows, then that will be true for you. This duality will exist in your experience. By the very nature of experiencing something, when you create something into being, the opposite also has to come into existence.

Papa Bray said that you do have a certain level of control over your experience of what that opposite is. Perception is projection says that it's along a spectrum, and that a certain amount is in your head, and a certain amount is outside. Right? So you have 100% control over the creation of any aspect of your perception that is totally inside your head, such as emotions.

When it gets to something like day or night, you're not going to be able to slow the sun down. It's going to set when it sets. You can have your own unique experience of time, like an hour-and-a-half break going by quickly or seemingly taking forever. But, we can't determine what time the sun's going to set. What Papa Bray said is if that bothers you, the fact that the sun sets at a certain hour, that's you. The sun doesn't care. It's going to set. The moon's going to rise. It's not going to worry about whether or not you're concerned.

Creation is really an understanding of the fact that we do live in a world of duality and dichotomies, and very few dichotomies are fixed in stone and unchangeable. The great philosopher Obi-Wan Kenobi showed this in Star Wars.

At one point, Luke confronts Obi-Wan and says, "Obi-Wan, you told me my father had died. You lied to me." But Obi-Wan responds, "No, I didn't. When the person your father was, Anakin Skywalker, ceased to be and he became Darth Vader, the old person who I knew and loved who was your father essentially died. So from my perspective, that was the truth." Then Luke says, "From your perspective." And Obi Wan responds, "Luke, you're going to have to learn something. Truth, in many contexts, is based on your point of view."

That scene gives you two really powerful ideas about the assumption of creation. The first is that you are in control of a certain aspect of what you believe to be true. The second is that other people can believe something else is true, and that's okay. It's okay for someone to come to me and say, "There's no such thing as higher self. It's all about God." I can switch gears, and we'll have a discussion about God. Or someone else might say, "To heck with this Huna stuff. I just want the straight Jungian self. Don't you dare bring in any Higher Self." No problem, we can talk about Self only.

One of my students grew up in a fundamentalist Christian household. As an adult though, he became interested in Eastern religions and philosophies which was especially upsetting to his mother. "After years of bickering about it and trying to get her to accept my way of thinking, it dawned on me that all I was doing was causing her great pain." Knowing about creation and the flow of dualities and dichotomies, my student started discussing things differently with his mother. He stopped emphasizing the differences in their views and started talking about their similarities. He recognized that his truth was not the only truth. His mother could keep her beliefs and he could keep his while still having good discussions and a positive relationship.

(!) SELF EXPLORATION:

1. What dualities and opposites have you set up in your life?

2. Can you see that others use different dualities? If so, how are they different than yours?

3. Think of someone whose opinions differ from yours (religion and politics are always good for this exercise!). Does it feel okay that this person keeps his/her own belief? Do you regard them as naïve/misinformed/insincere/just kinda stupid for disagreeing with you? Are you able to really listen as that person explains what he/she believes?

4: CYCLES AND RHYTHMS

The fourth basic assumption is cycles and rhythms. The assumptions are in that order: perception is projection, cause and effect, creation and, finally, cycles and rhythms. You need to get a working understanding of creation first because your cycles and rhythms flow between the opposites of creation. There is an undeniable experience of the energetic flow that moves back and forth between the opposites. Jung referred to it as a self-regulating system that is constantly seeking harmony.

It's pretty common to hear people say, "My life is out of balance." Technically, it's not. Life is never out of balance. But though life is never out of balance, you may feel out of balance because you've polarized yourself on one side. And if you really pay attention, I assure you that you can probably find where you are balancing that imbalance in another area. It might be a projection externally. For example, you may feel totally inadequate as a person, which propels you to work crazy hours at the office to "prove" yourself. You might feel guilty about lusting after someone else's wife so you are harshly critical of other people's infidelities. It might show up as a physical illness because you're unwilling to deal with certain negative emotions or limiting decisions. Nonetheless, as you understand the creation aspect of your dichotomy, there's a flow of energy that goes back and forth between your two opposites that you need to experience. If you try to avoid experiencing either of the opposites, it will still pop up somewhere in your life. Jung, Papa Bray, and anyone who has studied anything to do with the esoteric would say that this energy flow has three energies flowing around every dichotomy: starting, changing, and stopping.

So whatever it is that you've created as opposites, you will experience. If it's good and bad, you are doomed to experience good and bad. You will experience bad but that doesn't mean you will become bad. It means, by thinking that you're only good with no bad inside you, you may see more bad in the world.

Examples of this are all around us. What about those religious leaders or politicians who denounce certain lifestyles (i.e. promiscuity or homosexuality) who are then exposed as secretively living those lifestyles? They talk about the sanctity of marriage or the "sin" of being gay, and later we find out they're not just gay, but they're putting themselves in physical interactions that are dangerous. They're not just having one affair but many. And though they promise to change (usually after they've been caught), often they continue to bounce between whatever good/bad dichotomy they've constructed.

One of my students is a strong, intelligent, attractive woman. She couldn't understand why she kept getting involved with men who were manipulative and controlling. She also had an ongoing struggle with her finances. After doing a little digging, she realized that she had a strong dichotomy that centered around money. On one end of the spectrum, she identified herself as very independent and capable, the kind of person who really should be able to support herself. On the other end, she felt like money was scarce, that it was really hard to earn, and that she was incapable and needed someone to support her financially. The men she chose reflected that dichotomy about her relationship to money. They had the wealth she wanted (but felt she couldn't earn) but did not respect the strength she has. So she bounced back and forth between being in relationships where she was not respected but she was taken care of, and not being in a relationship, independent but broke.

Have you ever done that? You keep cycling back and forth between two poles. When I was 80 pounds heavier than I am right now, I used to cycle up and down and up and down. I cycled in rhythm back and forth between fat and not fat. I don't know why. I don't remember what my

46

dichotomy was. But I had a huge dichotomy between being healthy and not healthy. Every time I'd get to a point where I was healthy, I'd announce, "Man, I'll never be that big again." What happened shortly thereafter? I'd get big again. Living large on apple pie a la mode.

Jung said we are doomed to move back between these opposites. Jung focused on dealing with the Shadow and the anima and the animus (which we'll discuss in the second book of this series) to resolve dichotomy issues because those are the big ones. When you resolve the big ones, other, less critical opposites are easier to resolve. It's a trickle-down effect, especially if you deal with the Shadow.

When we see public figures act out and behave so differently from who they claim to be or what they claim to believe in, Jung would say is that they are playing out their Shadow. They're almost driven to play out the Shadow because they suppressed a part of themselves (one side of their dichotomy) that they didn't want other people to see. There's a level of denial that exists when you slide into the Shadow. But you're doomed to move back and forth between these opposites. It's not possible to do away with these opposites completely and you can't continue to hide from one side or the other. But you can be in control, at cause, for what you set up as your opposites. At the very least, you can control your experience of opposites even if you're dealing with opposites you can't control, like day and night.

We're not trying to get to one static state or a rigid place of balance, but a fluid balance, a harmony along the spectrum. It's like a seesaw, where you bounced up and down on either side as a kid. Think about it as if everything in existence is one of those teeter-totters. Up and down, day and night, light and dark, man and woman. I'm a good boy. I'm a bad boy. You have control over moving back and forth between many of these, and you have control over how you react to all of these, your experience of them.

You can create a sort of fluid union of some opposites along the spectrum, like between your masculine and your feminine side. With other dichotomies, like perfect son versus evil son, you can recreate it to be a different set of opposites, like pretty good son and not-so-good son. But even if you change your dichotomy, you'll still have that seesaw effect, and you'll still move back and forth between the two. The point is not about escaping that energetic movement. It's not about getting rid of the seesaw or some kind of static balance. The universe is always seeking balance. As soon as the seesaw hits a balance point, what happens? It pauses a moment in balance, and then the side that was up goes down and vice versa. This constant back and forth is just going to occur as part of life.

But you have total control over how you create those two, how you experience them. That's why Daddy Bray (Papa Bray's father) said the enlightened kahuna is able to hold conflicting views in mind without it causing conflict internally. They realize that these dichotomies cause internal struggle and conflict for others. Whenever I'm asked, "Don't you believe that people suffer?" my response is very simple: I believe that people suffer who believe they're going to suffer. I say this from my heart; I know that people do suffer. I have seen it, and felt it myself. What I am saying here, is that if you believe you NEED to suffer, do you increase or decrease your chances of suffering? (Hint: you increase your chances of suffering.)

Say that your experience of your past is, "Man, my childhood sucked. I wish I had someone else's childhood." My father had a fabulous quote (from a book by Claudia Black) that I didn't truly grasp until recently: "It's never too late to have a happy childhood." You can literally let go of your stuff, and you can look at your past in a totally different light. Life is only about suffering if we decide to make it about suffering. By the way, suffering has nothing to do with spirituality. But yet, if you make spirituality and suffering somehow link up in a dichotomy, you're going to flow back and forth between them. Bottom line: if there are people who don't suffer, and you're suffering, then it must be true that suffering, at some level, is controlled by your own perceptions.

By the way, a kneejerk I-want-to-avoid-really-becoming-empowered response to that is, "No, everyone suffers. If they say they don't, they're just in denial." That's just another way of avoiding having to be at cause. I've heard students say, "Well, maybe so-and-so just hasn't suffered really, yet. They will." Because suffering is in the dichotomy those students have created for themselves, they insist that it's there for everyone. The band Offspring has a lyric in their song, Self Esteem: "The more you suffer. The more it shows you really care. Right? Yeah." With that belief, what do you think they see in people?

One of my students brought his new in-laws to one of our workshops. This couple had been struggling financially for several years and had strong beliefs about why this was happening. "The economy is bad. There are no good paying jobs for older professionals. It's too late to start our own business at our age." The list went on and on.

During the workshop, we showed a video clip of a bunch of people throwing basketballs back and forth. Students are asked to count the number of times the ball is passed. During the clip, a guy in a gorilla suit walks right in the middle of the basketball players and waves at the camera. What's funny is that the vast majority of students are so focused on counting the balls that they completely miss this 6 foot gorilla. Check it out: (http://www.youtube.com/watch?v=vJG698U2Mvo).

For my student's father-in-law, that exercise was a huge break-through. It dawned on him that he was missing business opportunities right in front of him because he was so focused on "the bad news." "A former employer had been hinting he could use some consulting on a project, but I hadn't really been paying attention. All I had to do was give him a call." That following year, the couple was able to stabilize their finances simply by noticing possibilities that had been there all along.

YOUR PERSONAL TEETER TOTTER

If your dichotomy is set up as happy or sad, you have two choices: You can realize you have the ability to change that dichotomy, or you can just realize that, kind of like the tide going out, sometimes you'll need to be sad. Enjoy it then! Cry your eyes out. Have fun with it. Some people just love a good cry in the pillow. Personally, I don't. But people don't need to approach life the way I do to get the most out of it. Here's the deal, though. If you want to be cycling back and forth between happy and sadness, stop fighting it. Like the sun going down, if it's time to be sad, then just be sad. Wallow in your misery fully. Then, when it's time to let your sadness go, let it go.

50

This is a nonjudgmental approach to set up your dichotomies however you want. As with anything in your being – symbols versus signs, higher consciousness, the Shadow, the ego the persona – the point isn't to eradicate dichotomies. It's not some sort of Rambo approach to spirituality. There are always going to be dichotomies. Live with them. Enjoy them. But don't get used by them. Use them. Work with them.

I love the analogy of the surfer. I grew up on Oahu and on the north shore in the winter we can get waves that are 20, 40, even 50 feet high. When they're in the 20 to 30 range, that's called big surf. In some places, that's called a tidal wave. I have literally watched tourists flee in fear of their lives when they see these waves. At a certain point, the waves are so big that the lifeguards shut the whole beach down. But before that stage, good surfers can still ride them.

In some areas of life, you're just not going to be able to stop the waves from coming in. When it's time for big waves, you get big waves. I have no illusions. Spiritual paths like Huna aren't supposed to be used to try and eradicate those big waves. There's no chance to stop them. Instead, Huna teaches you to become the surfer who knows your beach, your waves, high tide, low tide, big waves, small waves. The objective is to learn how to ride the waves in such a way that you have a joyful ride in your life. It's either that, or you're going to be the tourist fleeing the beach. Oddly enough, it's your beach. It's your wave. It's your ocean. It's your ride. It's your choice.

(!) SELF EXPLORATION

1. Where do you feel that your life is in and out of balance? How might you change that?

2. How accepting are you of the dichotomies in your life (i.e. bad son vs. good son)? How easily do you move between them?

3. What is the story you tell about your childhood? How could you tell it differently?

5: LAW OF ATTRACTION

The fifth basic assumption is the law of attraction, a concept that is a laughing stock in some circles now. The concept itself is valid but too many people have jumped on the bandwagon and try to teach it without really understanding how it works. Frankly it doesn't work without the other basic assumptions in place. If you don't get that the world is your projection, if you're not at cause, if you don't understand creation, and if you've created the dichotomy that says you're doomed to cycle back and forth between happy and sad, no amount of positive thinking is going to stop the slide into sadness.

If you look at a foundation as having four corners (the four basic assumptions), the law of attraction is the filler between the four corners that brings those four aspects to solidity. The law of attraction can be applied to each of those corners. I once thought you had to learn this corner first, then this next, then that. But the truth is that you need to learn them all at once. I do believe that there is an order to the basics that helps them make sense and be useful. The order that I presented them in this chapter seems the clearest to most of my students. However, you need to really focus in on all of these basics at once and really incorporate them.

The law of attraction says that you will attract to you that which you hold in your consciousness. You will attract that which is similar to you. Angry people will create situations that make them angry. Sad people will experience situations that depress them. Fearful people will see hear and feel situations that scare them, and so on.

The law of attraction is just that simple: You call to yourself that which you hold inside you. The law of attraction does work. Though some people do teach the law of attraction and include the four other aspects, often the way it's taught is too vague and ambiguous – and ineffective.

Those who teach that you only need to hold a positive thought to call happiness to you are not doing anyone any favors. Affirmations done that way just don't work. To its credit, positive thinking can at least keep you open to possibility whereas negative thinking shuts you down completely.

But over 100 years ago, early psychologists discovered that positive thinking and positive-ness alone will not create the life you desire or make you into the person you want to be.

A classic example of this was James Mill and his son, John Stuart Mill. James Mill was a Scottish philosopher in the late 1700's and early 1800's. He believed that the mind had no creative function and the mind's process was a predictable mechanical response to external stimulations. So he thought that he could completely shape his son John's mind by rigidly controlling the stimulus he was given in early childhood. James Mill basically created the "perfect" environment for his son with everything that was happy, nothing negative. But the experiment backfired. By the age of 21, John suffered from deep depression. At one point, he almost committed suicide and went through his entire life experiencing periods of immense sadness[3].

People who believe in positive thinking might refer to the study of the Transcendental Meditation experiment in Washington DC. In this study, researchers took an army of experienced meditators into DC for several months and the crime rates dropped significantly. Through their thoughts, these meditators affected the energy field in DC. This energy fieled is what Rupert Sheldrake called the morphogenetic field. I've seen the reports on how they meditated and I still discuss the study when I present the fundamental principles of quantum-physics in some of my trainings. But those guys in the study were serious meditators. They weren't just thinking happy thoughts. They'd been practicing meditation for decades and were well armed with more knowledge than just the law of attraction. They thought positively, but they had 20 years of training going into it.

LAW OF ATTRACTION AND SELF-ACTUALIZATION

So, besides having the four basic assumptions in place, what does it take to make the law of attraction work? If you think about people you'd consider pretty together or self-actualized, don't those same people seem to have a handle on law of attraction? If so, it's because what is inside of them is all in agreement, not only their conscious thoughts but their subconscious minds as well. These people don't say that they want lots of money while harboring a subconscious belief that money is evil. They don't try to go after a relationship while fearing that they're unlovable. However

---

3 The unintentional benefit of this was that John Stuart Mill went on to develop more holistic theories about the mind and how it works.

they've gotten there, these people have integrated all parts of themselves and spend more time in the flow than others.

The law of attraction works all the time, not just when you're trying to use it consciously. So whatever you see in your life is a reflection of the beliefs inside of you, most often in the unconscious mind. When you're trying to invoke the law of attraction consciously, it's critical that you have the unconscious on board with whatever you are trying to attract. Without that agreement, your conscious desires will get sabotaged every time!

One of my students had finished our Master Practitioner's course in NLP (neuro-linguistic programming) and was starting his own practice. On his way to his first speaking engagement on the subject, he had a fender bender and had to reschedule. When the next scheduled time came around, he headed to the class and was sideswiped by another car. He rescheduled again. The third time, he was determined to teach the class. He got in his car and within the first mile he plowed into a truck and completely totaled his car!

Obviously, at this point, he stopped and asked what was going on. He finally realized that his unconscious was trying to protect him. He had an unconscious fear that he would fail as a speaker and that would end his new career. After he recognized and dealt with that fear, he went on to become a very successful speaker and coach.

(!) SELF EXPLORATION:

    1. What is your experience consciously using the Law of Attraction? Does it seem to work in some areas and not others? At some times and not others?

2. The Law of Attraction says that everything in your life is a reflection of what you are calling to yourself, consciously or unconsciously, intentionally or unintentionally. If that's true, just look around describe to see what you have been calling to yourself. Is it what you consciously desire?

SYMBOL VS SIGN

There's another basic concept that I want to mention briefly: the distinction between symbol and sign. This will be more important later when we delve into the subconscious mind so I'll cover it again in more detail in the next book. But since I see so much confusion around symbol and sign, especially as students become serious about their emotional/ spiritual development, I'd like to touch on it now. Jungian psychologists have spent a lot of time differentiating between symbol and sign though I don't think Jung himself spent much time on it. I take the Huna approach to this topic: There are signs, and there are symbols. The two labels aren't as important as the bigger-picture understanding of the difference.

At a recent workshop, some of my advanced students came to me: "Ah! There's a symbol! A symbol. Oooo! Did you see that symbol? I think the universe is trying to tell me something!!!" They walked me over to the window and pointed out a palm tree. It had a brown spot and it looked like something was leaking. My students asked, "What does it mean?" I said, "It means the palm tree has a spot." Some of them looked up at me and said, "No, really. What does it mean?" Who knows what it means? Maybe someone was walking by with something and bumped into it, and a little bit of sap came out. Who cares? Unless, of course, this spot on the tree evokes something in you.

A sign is a literal message of something. If an earthquake happens, that's a sign that a tidal wave may head to Hilo. No need to interpret. No need to analyze. Just make sure you have plenty of Spam and Vienna sausages on hand and a big bottle of water.

There are plenty of less dramatic examples of signs in everyday life. What about that big red sign with four letters S-T-O-P or when the traffic light turns red? You know to hit your brakes. Those are street signs, not street symbols. If they were street symbols, you would have to interpret them as you approached: Is this stop sign or light telling me to stop or to go?

In contrast, a symbol comes from the unconscious because the unconscious uses symbols, metaphors, emotions and even your physiology to communicate. Why? Because that's the language of the unconscious. Just like French is the language for people from France or sign language is the language that people who can't speak verbally use, the unconscious has its own language which happens to be symbols, metaphors, your emotions and your physiology. Sometimes these communications from the unconscious are pretty straightforward. Other times, the message comes in the form of a projection that begs for interpretation. For example, your unconscious could be offering a warning or a helpful hint about a decision you're trying to make. Or a symbol could be a message that your conscious behavior needs to be reconciled with an aspect of your unconscious.

One of my trainers, Gina, tells the story of a symbol that she ignored for a while. She was in a period of working really hard, and felt stressed and slightly overwhelmed. One day, her golden retriever Ginger broke a toe. The vet told Gina that there wasn't much they could do about it except make sure the dog stayed off her feet. But Ginger was really resistant. She fought staying down and kept breaking out of the pen Gina created for her.

A week or so later, Gina sprained her ankle in a snowboarding accident. Her doctor had the same advice for Gina that the vet had for her dog: "There's not much you can do about it except stay off your feet for a while." Gina was even worse than Ginger at taking that advice! On Christmas Day, Gina decided to try out her new carpet shampooer. Wearing flip-flops, she stepped onto the sudsy floor and slipped – spraining both ankles, fracturing one elbow and severely spraining the other! At that point, Gina asked herself, "Okay, so what are you trying to tell me?" The lesson was loud and clear: Gina needed to be more willing to ask for help. "Somehow, I'd gotten the message that asking for help meant I wasn't strong. And it was important to me to be a strong independent woman. Just like my dog who instinctively avoided showing weakness, asking for help made me feel too vulnerable. So what happens? I clobbered myself so I couldn't feed myself, dress myself, even brush my teeth! I had no choice but to ask for help."

Roughly, you can tell the difference between sign and symbol by your emotional response. If hitting a red light is no big deal to you, it's a sign. If you flip out every time you hit a red light, it's a symbol of something to you – but you still better hit your brakes! The trick, which we'll discuss in more detail later, is to treat sign and symbol appropriately and not confuse the two.

CONSCIOUS MIND

The conscious mind has two main components: the ego and the persona. Huna makes no distinction between the ego and the persona, but Jung was very careful to point out the differences between the two. Because the ego and persona have different roles to play on the path, I'll follow Jung's lead on this for discussion purposes.

Based on current measurements in neuropsychology and neurobiology, 90% to 95% of who we think we are is outside of our conscious awareness. Do you remember growing up and hearing that we use only 5-7% of our brain? Researchers are revising that belief. Now they say that we use all of our brain but we only use 5-7% consciously. It's not that we haven't tapped into 95% – we have. We're just not conscious of it. Neuropsychologists claim that there are more neurological connections in the body than stars in the sky or grains of sand on all the beaches on the entire planet! Clearly, we aren't in conscious control of all of that activity!

This assessment absolutely fits with the Jungian and Huna characterization of consciousness. Western thinking often approaches the mind as if the conscious is in control of the unconscious. But Jung and Huna would not claim that the 5% to 10% that is your conscious mind is in control of the other 90% to 95%.

In Jungian psychology and in Huna, most of the important work is done with and within the unconscious mind. If you only focus on working strictly with the conscious mind – the ego and persona – you usually won't get very far. If the conscious mind alone was all powerful, we could have talked ourselves to health, wealth and happiness years ago using our "conscious free will" through positive self-talk and affirmations. We tried that in the '70's and it didn't really work, did it? We just couldn't bludgeon our subconscious into submission no matter how many hours of affirmations we did! I don't want to knock the law of attraction or people who practice affirmations. I teach people how to improve their focus through language and thinking because there is a time and place for that. But it's a mistake to think that the ego alone can fix your life and get you where you want to go.

Time Magazine ran an interesting article in July 2010 citing research from Ruud Custers and Henk Aarts of Utecht University in The Netherlands as well as John Bargh of Yale University and Paul Gollwitzer of New York University. All of these researchers concluded that the subconscious has much more effect on our conscious decision-making and activities than previously assumed. In essence, they found that the whole notion of conscious free will is questionable. Free will actually seemed to be based in the unconscious rather than the conscious. Classic example: The smoker says "I should quit" while lighting up the next cigarette. If we had conscious free will, the ultimate book on how to live a perfect life would have been written by now. It would say, "Just think good, happy thoughts!" Done.

So if the important work happens in the unconscious and free will is not conscious but subconscious, why do we bother with the conscious mind at all? Actually, there are several good reasons why it's critical to get a good grasp on the workings of your conscious mind.

INTERWOVEN MINDS

Each aspect of your self has a particular part to play and all aspects of your self are intertwined. For instance, when someone pushes your buttons, what is activated is the Shadow or Anima/Animus. That pushes the Ego out of balance, which creates a Shadow effect, which pushes the button, which activates the Ego. To resolve issues with the ego and persona, you have to integrate the Shadow. Because of this, a lot of Jungian psychology books (though not Jung himself) start right off with the Shadow because it helps to balance the Ego and Persona because the Ego casts the Shadow. If we work on the Shadow, obviously we'll end up working on the Ego. Every part of who you are runs along a spectrum. On one end of the spectrum is persona; on the other end is higher consciousness.

The mistake is thinking that you are only one part along the spectrum and believing that's who you are completely. Both the Huna perspective and Jung's perspective agree that it's a self-regulating system. When there's an incongruency somewhere along the line between persona and the Self, the system will signal that something is out of whack. But the system itself doesn't care whether you ever right the wrong or resolve the incongruency. It's up to your conscious mind to decide whether to wake up and find congruency. Once the conscious mind has decided that, it has to work with all parts along the spectrum to resolve any incongruencies.

Western perspective

Another reason why I don't skip over the conscious mind is that our Western culture is very conscious-mind driven. It's such an important part of the way most people live their lives that to ignore it is like ignoring the internet. We live in a conscious world and we need to learn to work with it. We just aren't willing to see ourselves as a blob of unconscious yearnings and motivations with no choice in how we live our lives. We identify with "I think therefore I am." From Western psychology to Western business philosophy, the aim has been to gain conscious control of our environments, our reality.

As the researchers in the Time article point out, we may have less control than we think. But that doesn't stop us from trying! Especially in the West, our minds spend most of their waking hours consciously scheming, planning, analyzing. It's helpful to recognize that the conscious mind is not the dominant director of our lives, but to ignore its existence is a mistake as well.

Kill the Ego?

Several spiritual traditions acknowledge the conscious mind but say that the goal is to get rid of the ego entirely to attain spiritual mastery. Basically, they seek to obliterate the conscious mind to let Higher Conscious take control. But Jung and Huna would not buy into that perspective either. You can't eliminate the ego if you plan to stay connected to the rest of the world. You need your ego. You need to be able to work with and communicate with others. In fact, the idea of destroying the ego is, in my humble opinion, dangerous and crazy!

We have a consciousness for a reason. It's scary for me when I hear a spiritual leader saying we need to get rid of ego. Your ego is the part of you who says, "We have to get this ship going in the right direction." The Higher Self can be there to assist in a new balance but the Higher Self will not initiate the process.

I worry when a student says to me, "I'll just leave it all to Higher Self." I constantly remind students that your Higher Self doesn't care whether the marketing for your upcoming event goes out or whether you pick the kids up from school on time. Those things just aren't a function of the Higher Self. From a Huna perspective, the Higher Self is non-judgmental and loves you just as much whether you over-sleep or run a marathon in record time, whether you fool around a lot or live a life of celibacy. A lot of people think that the Higher Self wants to fix us and our lives. It doesn't. It's not that it doesn't want to fix it, and it's not that it does want to fix it. It's totally non-judgmental and non-interfering. However, keep in mind that non-interfering is different than non-responsive. The Higher Self does make suggestions and show aspects of the path that may be important. What I am saying here is that it won't interfere with the conscious mind's decisions.

CONSCIOUS MIND'S ROLE

Huna and Jung would say that the point isn't to eliminate your ego or persona. It's about making them pono and right with you, your capital S

Self. And most importantly, it's about understanding their proper roles and relationship to other aspects along the spectrum. We spend a lot of time in the Huna trainings to explain the role of your unconscious and the role of Higher Self. We also spend time on the persona and ego because it's important to understand the role of the conscious mind as well.

The conscious mind's main role is as the conductor of your orchestra.

Think about an orchestra: You've got the musicians and instruments that actually make the music. They have to work together and all play the same musical selection in order for the music to sound good. If they aren't on the same rhythm or if one musician plays a different tune or more loudly than the others, the result can be disjointed and awkward. Whether the orchestra chooses to play Metallica or Debussy the conductor's role is to keep the whole orchestra coordinated and in synch. But the conductor can't do it alone. The sound of his or her baton tapping at the beginning of the performance is pretty weak (and very quiet) compared to the power of the full orchestra!

So, one of the most important roles of the consciousness is as the conductor or the director. The unconscious mind and the Higher Self look for direction from the conscious mind. To many people, that sounds weird because we've been taught that the Higher Self should be above the ego. To become pono with all three selves and to have the Higher Self in its place above, the Higher Self and unconscious mind still look for direction from the ego.

I'll use an example to clarify: As I'm preparing to lead a specific kind of training, I have to clear my mind and focus in: "Okay, I'm going to be doing this specific kind of training here and this is the type of material I want to cover and here's the type of connection with Higher Self, the information that I want flowing." By the direction of my conscious mind, my unconscious mind and my Higher Self get on board and offer their wisdom as I deliver the training.

Often, when people are really good at what they do whether it is in sports or performance or art – or tax preparation! – they have done some process like this. They have lined up their subconscious and Higher Self to participate. They may not be totally clear on how they do what they do, but they have established the connection between the three minds. Like Milton Erikson, the famed American psychiatrist who was not able to explain how he established rapport with his patients, or athletes who find themselves in the Zone, or artists whose creation feels like it creates itself, the flow between the three minds can create seemingly magical results. This connection is actually the basis for success with the Law of Attraction, though often those who are good at applying the Law of Attraction don't realize its source. By connecting the three minds consistently, you get to a place where you are connected with Higher Self and you have resolved shadow and archetype issues. You complete the process of individuation, your foundation becomes solid and you become self-actualized. And it is all because your conscious mind directed your Higher Self and subconscious saying, "Clear your mind and focus on this and just do the initiation.

In many therapeutic contexts, the root cause of an issue often has to be made fully conscious before the problem can be dealt with. For example, one of my students, Dan, had a client who had tried every diet on the planet with no lasting results. She told Dan that her weight problems had begun not too long after her father had died. As Dan probed further, she explained that she had married outside of her religion years before. Her father was furious and completely disowned her, and the two of them had never reconciled. As she told Dan this story, she realized that her eating was a way of comforting herself over the loss of her dad, and a way of dealing with the guilt. By becoming conscious of the root of the pattern, she and Dan were able to successfully address her weight issues.

Another good example: One of my trainers, Nicholas, used to have warts on his hands that flared up periodically. He figured that they might have some unconscious emotional source but he didn't know what that source was. Applying some of the processes he's learned, Nicholas remembered an incident from his childhood: During a growth spurt when he was 9 or 10, Nicholas hit his head on a car door frame then hit the car seat in anger. His mother immediately admonished him: "Never show your anger like that! It's a small step between hitting that car seat and hitting your wife when you grow up." Can you imagine how that "truth" from his mother could affect a kid? From that day on, Nicholas never showed his anger – but warts popped out instead. When he became conscious of this, Nicholas was able to choose different ways to deal with anger and his warts have never come back.

The root of a problem often sits in the unconscious mind. When our conscious mind knows about this root, often that awareness itself clears up the issue. Even if it doesn't, by being conscious of the root, we can choose how to deal with it, what tools to use, what processes or practices to try. When we are conscious of the unconscious source of a problem, we have the insight and power we need to make a change. But if our conscious mind isn't aware of what the unconscious issues are, we can't know what is needed. The work itself may actually be done with the unconscious mind. But it's the conscious mind that will direct the work.

(!) SELF EXPLORATION:

1. How clear do you feel about the distinction between what is conscious and unconscious in your life? Between Higher Self and conscious mind?

2. What role has your own conscious mind played in your life? As the conductor? The dictator? Just along for the ride?

PERSONA

In Huna, ego and persona are lumped together as conscious mind. Huna recognizes the conscious mind as multi-faceted but just says that the conscious mind needs to be an accurate representation cross-contextually of the whole consciousness. Certain facets of the conscious mind are your thinking, how you interact with others. Huna says that the idea is to become [lokahi], to become united, consciously, so that your conscious mind is one unified mind. You are not necessarily fragmented (as in having different consciousness), but rather you do tend to consciously act one way at work and differently at home, one way when you're out partying with your buddies and differently when having coffee with your minister. In most instances, you don't recognize that you are acting differently. But if you step back and look at yourself, you can see that you are a different person in different contexts in many ways, even though it is all "you."

But I think lumping it all together can be a little too vague and ambiguous for most of us. Jung made clear distinctions between two facets of the conscious mind: ego and persona. And I think those distinctions are really useful.

Persona actually means "actor's mask" in Latin. Think of it like this: A persona is like the role an actor plays and the ego is the actor who plays those roles. A good actor may throw himself into a role but he knows that he isn't that character. The actor consciously plays his role and designs his character to fit into a particular scene or movie. Good actors can play all kinds of roles well. A poor actor may be limited or more one-dimensional.

Jung believed that a healthy ego relates to the world through a very "flexible persona." Like a good actor, a healthy ego isn't restricted to one type of persona but can shift according to the situation or context. So though you are always consciously the same "person," you probably act slightly differently at home than you do at work, relate differently to your parents than to your buddies.

The persona is like the outside of an onion: If you peel it back, you find the ego. So why don't we just drop the peels and relate to the world directly through our egos? Wouldn't that be more authentic? Sure, in the same way it would be more authentic to walk around naked. Interesting but definitely scary! In a way, the persona is like a protective coating. But in other ways, it's just a great way to relate to the world. You might wear a suit to a business meeting and shorts to a barbeque. Does that make you less authentic?

The truth is that you're always going to have a persona. The key is making sure your persona has a healthy relationship to the rest of you.

This process is not about eliminating your persona. In fact, in my humble opinion, any teacher who says, "Part of a spiritual path is getting rid of your ego and/or persona," is leading students down a very dangerous path. Your ego, your persona, is your consciousness. To get rid of them is the equivalent of lopping off your head. You have to have an ego. You have to have a persona. And this persona will be useful to you if it stays in a healthy relationship to your ego. Jung did believe that there are some dangers when the persona isn't in a healthy relationship to the ego. One danger he mentioned was that people can "become identical with their personas – the professor with his textbook, the tenor with his voice."[1] In other words, people can identify too strongly with the roles they play and forget that they are more than those roles. Think of the empty nest syndrome: parents become so identified with their kids' lives that they don't know what to do with themselves when their kids grow up. Or people who retire can feel useless and worthless without their career identities. Guys hitting forty might freak out because they can't play the young stud anymore! But when your ego is healthy, you know that these are just roles and that you are much more than the roles you play.

But our surroundings can make us forget that we're more than our persona. How many of you, when you first meet someone, say, "Oh, it's great to meet you! So what do you do?" Isn't that one of the first questions we always ask? "What do you do?" My answer is usually, "I'm a trainer." You may say, "I'm a doctor" or "I'm a homemaker" but do you notice how we respond? We make it into a statement of being

1 C. G. Jung, *Memories, Dreams, Reflections (London 1983) p. 416*

rather than a statement of doing. That's the persona. Answering a question of doing with a viewpoint on who you are. Rather than "I do training," my persona says, "I am a trainer." But the truth is that training is just something I do; it isn't really who I am.

Have you ever asked someone, "Nice to meet you – by the way, who are you?" I had a student ask me that once. He had thoroughly studied Jung. I looked at him and said, "How much time do you have?" I mean, how can I define that? And honestly, how many people even want to know who we really are? But while it may not be important for everyone you meet to know who you really are, it's definitely important that you know it.

Another persona issue is being rigid. Persona is like the hat we wear and most of us wear a lot of hats. But when our persona is not flexible, we don't change hats to fit the occasion. A guy who is demanding and authoritative at work may not be able to relax with his kids. A woman who is competitive on a sports field feels pushed to compete with her friends in social settings. A well-educated trainer insists on using sophisticated vocabulary during seminars – something I always discourage when I train seminar leaders. Someone once challenged me at trainer's training on this point. "Aren't you dumbing yourself down?" No. To me there's no point throwing out a word that people in the audience may not understand. It just means that you then have to waste time on teaching a vocabulary lesson to make sure people get the point. This would only make sense if part of your platform or persona is giving people a new word of the day. I teach at trainer's training that you shouldn't use big words to show how smart you are. Let how smart you are come out through the way that you do your presentation.

But this is an interesting point: When you change your vocabulary, are you really dumbing it down, or are you really getting into rapport with them and talking their language? It could be either. Of course, when I'm talking to my son Ethan, I have to put it in a way that a 12-year-old could understand it. But if you truly are dumbing it down and patronizing your audience, it won't feel good or right to do it. Imagine if I started doing my Huna training in Hawaiian – not that I could, I'm not fluent – just to show off that I can speak Hawaiian. That creates a disconnect. A healthy persona says: "I'm going to talk the language that my students can hear."

An intelligent individual might dumb down his or her language because in our society kids get beaten up for being too smart. It probably doesn't feel good to do this, which signals another kind of persona problem: a persona that is incongruent with the ego. It's not the action of the persona – in these examples, the language you chose to use – that makes you comfortable or uncomfortable. It's how well it aligns or not with the real you. When someone changes their language to relate better to others, it might just be a sign of a flexible persona. When they do it out of fear or disrespect, it probably won't feel right. The key is the feeling underneath the action.

A flexible persona means you can be appropriate within the context. When I get up in front of my students, I need to dress a certain way. My longtime students might say, "Matt, we love you for who you are. You can wear whatever you want." Really, could I do that? Could I show up on Saturday with a scruffy unshaven face and T-shirt on? Sure. But what would the reaction of the students who are not yet fully in control of their projections be? When I'm presenting to Fortune 100 clients, can

I show up in an aloha shirt? It might be all right in Nike on the West Coast, but maybe not with a major bank client on the East Coast. Being flexible enough to dress according to the situation just makes my work easier. And I'm pretty clear that I am not my clothes! So I can easily be flexible in my attire, the language I use, how I present what I teach. That said, do I take jobs that require me to fall into a persona that isn't in alignment with myself? No. For example, I've recently turned down a major television interview because the producer said I couldn't mention either Huna or NLP. For me, that's not about being flexible. That's about denying who I truly am.

It's a huge problem if the persona that you play is totally opposite of who and what you truly are. We see this pretty often in celebrities. To get what they want, they think they have to play a role that isn't really who they are. Often times, they end up playing out in private what's being suppressed in public. Or they see other people expressing the part of themselves they are afraid to express. Instead of respecting these other people for being who they really are, the person with the false persona shoots them down as if they are messengers of evil.

We have plenty of examples of this. Take politicians. The sad part is you can't get elected unless you fit a certain persona. So we literally have a political system built around lies and deceit. It would be refreshing for someone to get up and say, "This is who I am. This is my true nature. I'm going to be true to myself." They just wouldn't get elected. Instead, a politician may publicly demean gays then go out and have homosexual affairs. A bigot may pretend to be open-minded yet be a member of a secret hate group.

What about the world of spirituality? Have you ever seen a spiritual or a religious figure fall from grace? The truth isn't that "the higher you go, the harder you fall" but rather the farther you get away from your true self, the wider the gap between who you truly are and who you are pretending to be, the more drastically you will fall. We've seen spiritual leaders ranting about virtue while having multiple affairs or others preaching about the evils of greed while embezzling from their organizations.

With all of these people, the person they had to suppress became like a Tasmanian devil in their heads. Some get temporary relief and numbness in drugs, alcohol, or addiction. But when that doesn't work, they feel driven to do more and more, often becoming more and more bizarre.

Take someone like Tiger Woods, Bill Clinton, Kobe Bryant, John Edwards, and the list goes on and on. "He's such a smart guy. How could he do it?" The reason he could do it is that his true self became so frustrated with playing the role, the persona, of the good boy that the numbing, the abreaction, the polarity response had to, by its very nature, get bigger and bigger and bigger. With persona, that which is on the opposite end of what you portray, that which you push down and say is not you, gets shoved into the Shadow. When we get to Shadow, we'll discuss more about how persona and ego problems surface as shadow experiences.

It's not just celebrities who develop personas that don't fit. We often develop personas that don't reflect who we really are when we take our cues from the outside world. We think we have to act a certain way to be considered a good person in our culture or to make our parents proud. It can happen in a career. To keep our jobs or get ahead, we try to act in a way that doesn't really feel right. How many of you have just finally blown up in a career where you said, "I'm not going to play this @$%#! role anymore!"

Another good example is the closet eater. I once heard a story about this from a Huna student. Many years ago, another student had stayed with her on the way to coming to a workshop. The visitor was seen by other Huna students as a model of healthy eating. But the woman who was hosting her noticed that whole jars of peanut butter would just disappear. "I found wrappers tucked away in the trash can. An entire tray of Oreo cookies was gone one night. And I thought I was just nuts until I found things in her bedroom." The visitor's persona of "healthy eater" hid the part of her that craved junk food!

To have a healthy, balanced ego, you need to get rid of any persona that is out of alignment with who you are. I'm not saying you will eliminate your persona totally. I'm saying that you will develop a persona that aligns with who you are. It may not be exactly 110 percent, but your persona has to be in alignment with the Self, with who you truly are. When it is aligned, the persona no longer has the need to shove any Shadowy experience into your face, into your realm, into your existence.

Life can get pretty scary if an out-of-alignment persona is built up big enough. I know this from my own experience because I once had to face the fact that I may lose the ability to teach Huna if I didn't get my persona on board.

The story centers around my first marriage. To everyone on the outside, my first marriage looked pretty perfect. But at the level of persona, I was just playing the role of great husband for my friends, for my family. I knew it wasn't quite right, especially as I got deeper into Huna and began teaching it. But I couldn't imagine ending the marriage and facing the hurt and disappointment from the people around me. My friends all looked to me for advice in their relationships and, as I talked to them, I'd think, "Who am I to say this?" Sound familiar? That's a persona that has taken on a life of its own. That is a persona that is not true to who and what you are.

One day in a training, I heard my father talk about 'oia'i'o (which means to be truthful, authentic, genuine). "You need to be truthful." I had to get up and walk out of the room. I began to hyperventilate. It hit me hard: "How can I get up in front of a group of people, and teach 'oia'i'o, one of the most basic concepts in Huna and aloha[2]." I had been teaching truthfulness to my students, but I hadn't been truthful to myself. "As much as I love Huna, as much as I love what I do, I cannot continue doing it knowing what I know now."

So I either had to give up teaching Huna or give up the persona I had built. I had to be willing to face the repercussions of so many years not being true to who and what I am. I had to be willing to accept having put so much energy and invested so much time in this persona. I had to be willing to accept whatever the fall from grace there was going to be.

---

2 Aloha is more than just a greeting. It's state of being that includes compassion, unity, humility, love. I discuss the meaning of aloha in The Foundation of Huna.

In a matter of weeks after that, my relationship began to fall apart. As soon as you have a glimpse of the truth, your prior foundation starts to crack. A piece falls off. You try to patch it. Then the next piece falls off. The whole thing just starts to crumble. I was sure my family would throw me under the bus. Friends told us that we couldn't divorce, even after I explained that I'd been living a façade for 5 years. In the end, my family was forgiving and my friends figured it out. But it was rough.

So I know what it is like when you have built up a persona to be so big that your entire reality is based around it. Your entire existence is dependent on your persona and it's so tied into so many things that you do. We have so many public examples in our modern history of people who have not been true to themselves and we've seen them fall. Yet we tend to think, "That will never happen to me. I would never be that silly." I assure you that if that's what you think, you're in denial. It can happen to any of us when you let the persona become so far away from who and what you are. And letting go of that persona isn't easy. I've experienced this in a relationship, in a job, in health and fitness. When my persona wasn't aligned with the real me, I was just playing the game, going through the motions. In some ways it felt good, safe. But I assure you that when your persona is aligned with your true self, it feels so much better.

The idea is not to get rid of the persona. The idea is for the persona to be congruent with the ego and an accurate reflection of your true Self. It can never be who you are. Your persona, by its very definition, is in the realm of consciousness. It is a conscious decision to look, sound, feel, act, and behave a certain way. It can never, by definition, be your true, authentic self. All it can be – and this is the key – is an accurate reflection of your true, authentic Self.

Sometimes people choose a role because they think it will make them more effective. A police officer might think he has to play the tough guy. A manager might think she has to be friendly and outgoing. A lot of trainers think they have to be theatrical. Personally, I decided that I need to be just who I am both on stage and off. I may slow down the energy a little bit when I'm training, but not as a persona thing. The slowing down is about getting into the flow, but it still feels authentic. On the other hand, people have told me that I needed to start wearing a suit when I'm teaching Huna because that's what students will expect. I won't do it because it feels too far away from a reflection of my true Self.

A terrific trainer, Kathy Singh, came here to teach at the upper levels of Huna. She is very flexible with persona and says, "I'll routinely get up in front of groups that I don't know and I'll ask, 'What do you need me to be in order for you to have the best experience of this training? Do you need me to be a Buddhist, a Catholic, a Muslim, a Hindu, what? I'll be whatever you want me to be, just so you have the best experience of it.'" To get her message across, she's totally willing to switch gears and speak whatever language her students can hear.

The healthy persona needs to be a reflection of true Self but it allows us to play different roles that fit the context. The other day, my daughter looked at me and said, "Daddy, I love you, and you are my best friend". As a dad, my heart just warmed up. Wow, did that feel good! However, I had to explain to Skylar, my 4-year-old, "Sweetie, I love you. I love hanging out with you. I'm your dad. I'm not one of your buddies. You and I can't be just like buddies. There needs to be a certain boundary with parents and children. We can be friendly, play, and hang out but I'll always be your dad." Skylar started pre-school a few months before writing this book. Sometimes, she comes home and tries to run the games that she runs with the other kids at school.

For example, she wanted to play one afternoon. I had to remind her, "Honey, I'm your dad and right now I'm working. When I finish, then we'll play." "No, Daddy, you need to come now!" which apparently works with the kids in school. I said, "We're not in school; we're at home. You don't call the shots here." "So, who does?" Of course, I had to tell her the truth: "Mommy!"

There is a persona, a role that you're going to play in every area. It's not totally who you are but one reflection of who you are. It's like a snapshot that is true and an accurate representation of your Self. You're clear that the snapshot is not truly, totally who you are but it also can't deny the truth of who you are. So when I do a corporate training, I'll put the suit on. It doesn't matter to me. When I'm booked for a television show, I ask, "Would you like me to wear a suit, or can I wear an aloha shirt?" If they say, "We'd appreciate it if you could wear a suit," I'm fine with that. But if they say "And we'd like it if you didn't mention the word Huna," I tell them that I'll have to pass on the interview. Why? Because what I wear doesn't matter. But to deny my path would be to deny my Self.

Persona is an act. You'll never be satisfied with just the act but it can be downright painful if it doesn't align with who you are. When I was still with my ex, we'd spend time with our friends and family and I could play the role perfectly. But on the way home, I'd feel awful. If you're playing a phony role at work to get ahead, people might be totally impressed with your performance. But as soon as you get home, you just want to scrub that false, slimy persona off of you.

By the way, when the persona feels like a well-fitted, amazing, beautiful outfit, it is true to the Self. It's like you don't want to take it off. My grandmother once told me, "Matt, relax. You're not on stage right now." My wife Soomi turned to her and said, "Grandma, he's always like this." Grandma's response to Soomi? "I'm so sorry, sweetie."

(!) SELF EXPLORATION:

1. Think about the various personae you have adopted in your life.

2. How would you describe each one?

3. How authentic, close to your true self, does each feel?

4. How well do they serve you?

5. And for those personae that don't feel authentic, what changes could you make?

6. What new persona might you enjoy trying on?

EGO

Ego is sometimes referred to as the king or queen of the conscious mind. It is the part of you that says: "I know what I know and I'm clear about it." It thinks rationally, analyzes and plans. It sets goals and directs our focus and attention. A healthy ego is a very good director that knows exactly what to do in every situation and how to involve the Higher Conscious and subconscious. So the ego is absolutely essential. We've made the word ego evil, dirty, or nasty. Big mistake. We have to shed that misperception.

That said, I can see where the misguided idea of "eliminating" ego to find Self came from, even though I think it's a very dangerous concept. If the ego is out of balance, it can definitely create problems, especially when it believes that it is the whole enchilada of who you are.

A swami told me a story from the Hindu tradition when I was 8 or so. He said that Brahma, the Creator of the Universe, was burned out and needed a vacation. (I am sure the story is much more poetic than this, but this is how my 8 year old mind heard it.) So he decided to go to earth and take the embodiment of a cow. But after a while, all of the gods and goddesses looked around and didn't like what they saw. Without Brahma, things weren't running so well. So they searched the Universe to find out what the heck had happened to him.

Finally, they found Brahma as the cow and they said, "Dude, you've got to come back to work. The Universe needs you." But the cow just looked up at Shiva, Krishna and the gang and said, "I don't know who the heck you're talking to. I'm a cow. Look, here are my calves. I've got mud all over me. Creator of the Universe? Are you nuts?"

This went on for a while with the gods and goddesses trying to convince him and Brahma insisting that he was a cow. Finally, one of the gods, probably Kali, got fed up. So she pulled out a sword and lopped the cow's head off. Immediately, Brahma popped out as himself saying, "Wow! I really am the Creator of the Universe." And he went back to work.

The point of the story is that we sometimes get trapped in the ego where we think what we have is real, where we think what we have means something. We've forgotten who we really are and deny other parts of ourselves. Sometimes on our path we do feel like cows or pigs or any animal... We feel like we're rolling around in the muck. Yet we each carry inside us that ability to create our universe, though we've somehow forgotten that.

Healthy vs. Unhealthy Ego

So what is the ego? According to Huna, the ego is your conscious mind. It is your rational thinking. It's the analytical aspect of who you are. Sounds pretty benign, right? But we live in a world where rational thinking has become the standard or norm of intelligence. The person who is able to think things through and override those "silly" emotions is considered to be the most wise. "Gut feeling? Must be indigestion, acid reflux! Gut instinct? Just some primal holdover from caveman days. Dreams? Just something that happens when you're snoring – they don't mean anything."

As I mentioned, the ego is important. But when out of balance, the ego doesn't acknowledge the validity of the subconscious or Higher Conscious. The Ego can be balanced or unbalanced, healthy or unhealthy, meaning that it can serve you on your path or create obstacles for you. Though "eliminating" the Ego is a dangerous concept, balancing an ego that is unhealthy can be very helpful because an unhealthy ego will sabotage all your attempts at growth and self-empowerment.

So what makes an unhealthy ego? As Maslow's research pointed out, characteristics like being greedy, self-centered, mean-spirited, arrogant are unhealthy. Most of us would agree with that list. But another big sign of ego imbalance is constant self-doubt. For example, I have a few students who have experienced pretty advanced levels of energy work. One particular student, a great individual, sends me emails all the time that say, "I'm still not feeling the energy. I still don't know whether or not this is true." His conscious mind, his ego, hasn't found the proof it wants. So I tried to remind him of his successes with the energy: "One of your clients came to my weekend training and talked about how powerful you are because your energy was just flowing and..." He interrupted me and said, "Yeah, I know. But I haven't felt it yet." He's trapped in self-doubt because his ego isn't convinced of what the rest of him knows to be true. An unhealthy ego can constantly doubt who and what you are, your abilities, your talents, your wisdom. An ego can be relatively balanced yet still get thrown off. For instance, when you're learning something new, you might sometimes feel like you're in flow. Everything's going well and you feel solid. Then suddenly, you question. That questioning is the ego stepping in.

Another example of self-doubt: Your gut screams, "Go left! Go left!" but your conscious mind refuses to listen and demands that you go right. Your ego feels that it must be in charge and, because it can't grasp the wisdom and insight of your unconscious and Higher Self, it insists on calling the shots based only on data that can be consciously known. It overrides all other aspects of what and who you are. This too is an ego that is out of balance, unhealthy.

In contrast, a healthy ego has a calm certainty. People with healthy egos can be strong without being pushy or rude. My teacher Etua is a good example. When a beginning student tells him, "You know, Kumu, I think it would be better if we did hula in this way," Etua gently explains that he's in charge. And he re-explains that he's in charge just as gently on the second and third day if necessary. That's a healthy ego. Etua knows who he is and knows what role he needs to play in order to accomplish something. Etua's ego flows from Self, not vice versa. The Higher Self, while not making decisions for the conscious mind, still directs it. We'll get into this concept in later books. For now, it's enough to remember that the ego is not above but below the Higher Self.

The people who were mentioned as self-actualized in books by Robertson[1], Maslow, and Jung all had healthy egos. I really don't see any of these individuals acting as floor mats, letting others walk over them. From one perspective, it might seem as if "Wow, those people really think highly of themselves." They all did – all from a humble, congruent foundation.

As Papa Bray put it, a healthy ego has truthfulness: "This is who I am and this is what I do. These are my boundaries." A healthy ego has a strong foundation of ha'aha'a. Ha'aha'a basically means humility or humbleness. It doesn't mean groveling or self-doubt or a lack of assertiveness. But it means that you come from your heart in a very humble way.

A healthy ego has a strong internal check on what you are doing and who you are, like an internal honesty factor. It asks itself questions like: "Is this the best I can do?" "Is this the right action at this time?" Though listening to feedback from the outside can be important as well – the response from an audience, the questions from students, the critique from a trusted advisor – an unhealthy ego will ignore internal knowing

1 Robertson, R. (1992). Beginner's guide to Jungian psychology. Lake Worth, FL: Nicholas-Hays, Inc

and look primarily to the outside for guidance: "What would make them like me more?" "What do the cool people think and say about this?"

But though a healthy ego does a great deal of internal checking, it does not assume that there is nothing to learn from the outside world. An ego out of balance believes that no one else knows better than it does, that it knows right from wrong better than anyone else.

In some of my beginner workshops, I've had people accuse me of claiming that my path is the one and only true path. No matter how many times I say, "This is my path and I'm sharing it with you from my heart," people seem to misunderstand or delete, distort, and generalize what I say. "What do you think? You think this is the only path?" Well, no, I don't. I think it's the right path for me and I'm committed to it. But I know that there are other paths that are valid and right for others. I teach people that I am less interested about their attraction to Huna than in their coming to a realization that they need to pick a path and go down it. Picking a path doesn't make all the other ones wrong; it means you have found what is right for you.

But, I have to admit, at one point, when my ego was out of whack, I did think that my path was the one and only true path. I was 12 years old and I had just walked over burning coals in a workshop. This was an incredible experience that helped me breakthrough boundaries and opened my eyes to what is possible in the world. I just knew that, from then on, nothing could stop me! And with all the vast wisdom of a 12 year old, I went to see my grandfather. I explained to him how the world works and what we are capable of and what it all means. I told him that I was now invincible! I just had to focus on the positive and my universe would be perfect! My grandfather listened very patiently then asked, "And how long have you known all of this?" It had been about 4 days. Very calmly, he said, "Well, can I just give you some other ways of thinking?" Without arguing or telling me I was wrong, he shared from his wisdom of many years and many experiences: "There are things on this planet that you sometimes do have to face. A hurricane will come and the waves can get pretty big on the north shore of Oahu. And unless you have experience surfing them and listen to others who have surfed them before, it's not the smartest thing to just jump right in and think you know each and every wave. A new wave you've never met can suddenly slam you."

I argued back hard. I was sure that I knew it and I knew it all. He looked at me very lovingly and said, "Matt, you're only twelve. You'll learn a little bit more along the way!" But I didn't want anything to do with that. I had just walked on twelve feet of burning hot coals and, by god, that meant I could do anything in the face of anything! But my grandfather wanted to make sure I didn't walk out into the street thinking that I could transcend through the bus – because he was pretty sure the bus would win.

That's a great example of an unhealthy ego. No matter what age you are or what place you're in, if you think, "I know it all!" then you're in trouble. An unbalanced ego closes the door and says, "I got it. I got it all. I'm done." A religious group can have an unhealthy ego that says: "Ours is the one and only true path. It cannot be questioned." A culture with an imbalanced ego would approach other societies with the attitude that these societies must conform to the "modern" or "civilized" way of thinking and acting, as many Western cultures have done historically. A teacher with an unhealthy ego might claim, "I had this great epiphany. There are three steps to enlightenment and they are guaranteed. And I came up with them. No one else did." These people won't give anyone else credit and they slam other teachers and paths. Does that sound like the perspective of a healthy, truly self-confident ego?

In general, a balanced ego will, as Uncle George Na'ope put it, realize that not all wisdom is in his or her school. Your school of thought is just that – your school of thought. It's for you. Here's what works for me: I know what I know. Someone else may know something different than I know or think in a different way, and that's perfect for them. That's just fine. Do I want to argue? Not nearly as much as I wanted to argue in the early days, before I worked to balance my ego.

For example, a few years back, I taught a workshop in Toronto and made the statement that smoking doesn't cause cancer. By the way, there's no causation between smoking and cancer. Smoking weakens certain parts of your body and can accelerate disease, but cancer is definitely not just a physical thing. Medical doctors are beginning to realize that, the mind/body connection – you know, that whole mind/body thing. I heard it's catching on.

So a guy at the workshop challenged me. I laid down a great position on this with all the material and research that I knew at the time. He shook his head and said, "I just don't believe that." I took a deep breath, exhaled, and said, "Okay. You hang onto that belief then. Next question?"

No emotion, no charge on it. My response floored him. The same guy came to a Huna workshop a couple of years later. He walked up, gave me a big hug and said, "That was the absolute best thing you could have done – just completely flat on your response to me. No anger, no sadness, no nothing. You just let me be."

Everyone is entitled to his or her own belief. A person with a healthy ego offers his or her belief like a handshake: they offer it but don't force it on anyone. As my father used to warn me that the life of doing seminars and trainings can be very frustrating. You walk into a room and say, "Here is a gift (or ho'okupu in Hawaiian) that can change your life. You can let go of your negative emotions, etc ..." I've seen people who've been in therapy for over ten years who come to a workshop, experience one of the techniques for about 8 minutes and their negative emotions absolutely dissolve. And yet we're fortunate if 30% of the room says: "I'd like to know more."

For example, one of my students researched the Time Empowerment® Techniques we use and used Cognitive Behavioral Therapies (CBT) for a control group. The Time Empowerment® allowed for a complete reduction in depressive symptoms in just 5 sessions. It took 13 sessions for any reduction with CBT. And with the CBT group there was a 29% relapse rate and a 11% re-hospitalization rate. With Time Empowerment® there was no relapse at all. With those kinds of results, wouldn't you think everyone on the planet would want to learn more? Nope.

It's "okay if people say, "It's just not for me." But it can be really frustrating to offer your teaching like a gift, then to have some people spend more time trying to knock it out of your hand than to receive it. I know these techniques work and that many if not most of these concepts are valid. But the doubts of the Ego are sometimes in the way.

David Shephard, a student of Huna who also taught at our workshops and added much value to our school in Hawai`i, said that most trainers focus on the showmanship of training, a "Look at me, look at me" as a way to win over the crowd. Dave believed in the approach of 1) have the audience learn something, 2) show them what they just learned, and 3) have them do what they just learned. The audience will be amazed at how powerful they themselves are, not how great you are. He felt that should be the goal of a trainer.

As for me, I know what I know. As an author and a workshop leader, my job isn't to impress you with who I am. My job – and the job of every mentor, coach, parent or teacher as far as I'm concerned – is not even to impress you with who you are. It's to assist you in seeing how empowered you are. That's a healthy ego, and it's especially important if part of your path is to teach other people. To guide other people you have to have a healthy, unshakable ego that comes from the heart with a strong foundation in ha'aha'a (humility) and the realization that all you can do is share your mano'o, which means your thinking or truth.

A healthy ego is comfortable with what it knows – and also what it doesn't know. For example, I was teaching a training in San Diego once and a student asked me a complex question. I answered and right on point.

I could tell that the whole audience got it immediately. A guy came up to on break and said, "Man, you answered that one with some authority!" And I said, "Because it was a question about my foundation of what I know. This is what Huna would say. I'm sure other paths might say it in a little bit of a different way. However, this is it for me."

After lunch that day, someone asked me a different question and I literally said, "There's no way I can answer that. That question is off my foundation. I don't know the answer. You're asking me a question that's outside of my scope of knowledge." I learned to be clear about what I know and don't know from Uncle George Na'ope. When you would ask Uncle George a question about Hula or Hawaiian studies, the answer was very definite. But when you asked him something that had nothing to do with what he knew, he'd shrug and say, "Why are you asking me?"

Though the balanced ego realizes that not all wisdom is in one school [a'ohe pau ko iki i ko halau], its goal in life is to not learn everything.

An unhealthy ego may feel like it needs to know everything, but a healthy ego has "dedication." This comes from the Hawaiian concept that, on a spiritual path a healthy ego is also a dedication. Within this dedication is the concept of aho nui which means to have patient perseverance on this path. For years, I've said to people part of becoming a Kumu Huna (teacher of Huna) means to dedicate to that path. It means that I'm not doing anything else. For instance, there may be a Reiki energy healing class in town. Though I am dedicated to practice Huna and that's all I do, if someone comes along who has a very wonderful, magnificent and beautiful lineage, I might share knowledge to enhance my path. But I remain dedicated to the path that I know is for me. I wouldn't skip Huna because Reiki looks cool, but I would learn from Reiki to enhance my chosen path. A healthy ego knows that anything is possible and everything is real and millions of different truths can exist, but you've found the one that works for you. You have found the path that is right for you. And nothing and no one can shake you from that path. I share my path with hope that you grab some ano'ai, some seed, and that you can plant that and allow it to bear fruit.

When your ego is balanced, the focus is no longer needing to know everything, but on knowing who you are, knowing yourself, bringing in a healthy dose of ha'aha'a (humbleness and humility) and realizing that anyone you meet on the path may be just as far along or even farther down the path than you. And the healthy ego doesn't compare or feel inferior or superior to other paths or because of where it sits relative to others on its own path. The one thing a healthy ego really aims to know is just one thing – yourself. In the film The Matrix, Neo walks into the place where the young rebel humans are training in superhuman powers. Neo's mentor, the Oracle, points up above the door and says, "You know what that says? It says, 'Know thyself.'"

Another sign of a healthy ego is that it knows when it needs help. It knows its strengths but it's also clear about its weaknesses and is not afraid to admit them! A balanced ego doesn't need to be right in everything and have all the answers. A person with a healthy ego seeks expert advice and assistance, whether it's from a medical doctor, a professional consultant or a good plumber. A person with a healthy ego won't try to do everything alone. A friend of mine is the classic example of this kind of ego imbalance. Not only does she think that she has to be the perfect wife, mother and daughter, but she also feels driven to maintain a demanding career – all without any assistance. To her, asking for any kind of help or advice has come to mean failure. And she's not alone. I see a lot of women today who seem to believe that they are supposed to be Superwoman and that's unfortunate.

My mom had a plaque on her desk that said "The best man for a job is often a woman". My wife is similar to my mom, in that she is amazingly confident, runs the business, and knows her boundaries. Both are super women, but neither thinks they are Superwoman. My mom still wants me to open the door for her and show her that I am a gentleman. My wife asks me for help when she wants to exercise or take a break from the kids. They don't believe that being an empowered women means giving up relaying on others for help. In fact, I have learned from both of them that a truly empowered woman (and man for that matter) is one who is super and also knows that others are just as super and can help.

Personally, I didn't last long as Superman! I got to a point in my career years ago where I realized that I couldn't do everything myself. There are some things that other people are better at than I am, and there are other things that, though I can do them pretty well, they aren't the best use of my time. Fortunately, by the time I recognized this, I'd done some ego-balancing in my work life. I was able to face my needs and weaknesses as well as figure out my priorities. Most importantly, I was able to let go of certain tasks and ask for help from others.

My alaka`i (right hand man, or woman in this case) at Huna, Karen, now does much of what I'm not good at. One day, I said to her, "You have accepted the job of [Alaka'i]." She asked, "What does that mean?" "That means I know who I am. I know what I'm good at and I know what I'm not good at. And I need you, Alaka'i. I need to be able to not only rely on you to teach the classes when I'm not available, but also I need you to help me organize certain things."

The healthy ego doesn't think that any task is beneath it – or above it. The healthy ego knows its path and what it should be doing on that path. This is another prime role of the ego: Once your path has become evident, you know what you're meant to do. No matter how big or small the job, it's all the same to a healthy ego. Karen is an example of this. So is Dr. Saba, who works with me at The Empowerment Partnership. Dr. Saba is considered as one of the foremost, if not one of the top two or three, experts on information technologies and instructional design. I'm in awe of some of the things that he has experienced in his life and some of the people that he's worked with. Yet he'll do whatever we need him to do, and remains extremely humble and easygoing. If you ask him a question about technology, he always starts it off with: "Well, in my little simple world of how we do things . . ." I always jump in to correct him: "You mean, as the god of information technology?" "No, Matt, you're overstating my role in the universe."

When an ego is healthy, it has a healthy dose of ha'aha'a – humbleness. To me, humbleness and humility are what help to keep a healthy ego pono. When you are confident about who you are, what you know and your foundation yet you are equally ha'aha'a (humbled) by others' knowledge and brightness, then you have an ego that is healthy. To be truthful and to be humble (oia'i'o and ha'aha'a) means that you know what you know – and you also know that the more you know, the more you realize you don't know.

It's also possible for an ego to be pretty balanced in one arena and not so healthy in another. For example, I've mostly had a pretty balanced ego when it comes to spirituality and a lot of humbleness. But for a long time, I was much more ego-driven in my career. I was a "my way or the highway" type of manager early on, believing my thinking and way of doing things was the only correct way. I know other people who are relaxed and genuine in front of large audiences but uncomfortable and self-conscious at social gatherings. Some people are able to relate calmly and objectively with friends, but get defensive and crazy in family relationships.

So ego balance can be contextual. Everyone has a different path. The good news is that you can learn from the ego balance you experience in one arena and bring it into another.

(!) SELF EXPLORATION:

It's sometimes hard to spot our own egos when they are out of balance. Try answering these questions:

1. How do you feel when someone disagrees with you? Comfortable? Defensive?

2. How do you feel when you don't know the answer to something?

3. How do you feel when someone questions your authority?

4. When others compliment your performance, do you feel like a fraud, undeserving?

5. How often are you willing to step out of your comfort zone, into unchartered territory?

6. Can you remember times when you ignored your gut feeling or intuition? How did that turn out for you?

RELATIONSHIP TO HIGHER SELF

Though the ego directs the activity of the subconscious and Higher Self, a healthy ego allows itself to be guided by the wisdom and insight of Higher Self. That's why spiritual teachings teach that the Self, or the Higher Self, has to be above the ego. I discuss Higher Self more fully in other works but here I'll focus on ways you can recognize if the ego does not have the proper connection to Higher Self.

Stagnation is a primary symptom of an ego that is not guided by Higher Self. The Higher Self offers unlimited potential and growth within any chosen path, and because it does, the healthy ego doesn't have to get into the grass-is-greener-somewhere-else mentality. The grass is greener, in my opinion, because people are not being guided by their Higher Self. They aren't tapping the ever-evolving wisdom of Higher Self so get stuck where they are. And when you get stagnant on the path and graze in one area for too long, you eat all the grass in that particular spot! If you'd just let your Higher Self take you one more step down your path, you'd find a new patch of grass on your chosen path.

Human potential trainers and spiritual teachers can get caught up in this. They stumble upon a really good teaching or path, maybe a message from Higher Self. But they don't recognize its source so the ego begins to take credit. "Look at me. I've come up with this amazing system!" They may even believe that their students can't progress without their personal input. Twenty years later, these teachers and trainers are still promoting the same message. They'll repackage it and call it something different. And, honestly, some of these people are brilliant. But when you make anything about you, about your ego alone, a stagnation occurs. This is true in all areas of life: health and fitness, relationships, career.

A healthy ego is guided by the Self and a healthy ego has its right place under the Self, but not as a servant. Never is the relationship between the Self and the Ego a servant/master relationship. It simply isn't in the Self's nature to act as "master." However, an ego that is out of balance might try to treat the Self and the subconscious as slaves. How would that show up? In health for instance, the ego may say, "I want my body to give 110%. I need the energy to be able to do all the things that I want to do. But when I go home, I'm going to get wasted and stay up until 1:00am, wake up at 4:00am, and start this whole cycle all over again. I am in total control over my body!" The ego tries to push the other 90% of yourself beyond its limits. That is a definitely a master/slave-type approach!

But the Self or Higher Self will never do that. It will guide the ego but without attachment to outcome. It never seeks to "punish" the ego for not following its guidance and it never pushes the ego, subconscious or physical body to do anything. The Self knows that all parts of yourself need to stay pono.

Frankly, when the ego tries to be the slave master over your life to drive you to a certain result, it doesn't work out in the long run. One of my personal examples is my prior struggle with weight. Initially, I worked to get healthy and lose weight because I worried about how my students looked at me. I was basically doing it for ego, or more accurately, persona. So I tried a dozen different health and fitness programs thinking my shoulders had to be a certain size or my waist had to be a certain size so that students would accept me. I would have some success but guess what happened as soon as I stopped training or hit a plateau: A stagnation of taking care of my health occurred and I backtracked. I slid back into unhealthiness and gained back whatever weight I'd lost. It was that self-regulating seesaw, teeter totter, back and forth: healthy/unhealthy, losing weight/gaining weight. I couldn't maintain healthy habits because I was doing it to feed the ego – not for my path, my true self, to be true to who I am.

Finally, I realized that I had to resolve a bunch of ego and persona issues (along with some work in areas of the unconscious that Jung called the Shadow). As a teacher and trainer, you always have the opportunity to work on ego, persona and shadow. As soon as I thought I knew enough (ego) I would get brought back down to earth. As soon as I attempted to be someone I wasn't on stage (persona), someone would see through it. And when either was out of balance, I would see it in my students and hear myself saying, "I'd never act like that" (Shadow!!!).

I have been there and done that, so I always malama (cherish) my students and tell them, "You are doing the best you can with the resources you have!" When they share something with me, I will often tell them, I have gone through tough times too. My five-year-old daughter Skylar has a saying (and please feel free to quote her) "You don't have to be perfect, you just need to do your best." All I have done with my ego, persona and shadow (which we will be covering in the next book) is to do my best with resolving the issues and letting go of my "stuff."

After doing that, I was able to get on a program and stick with it. I've been able to exchange unhealthy habits for healthy ones. I've maintained my weight, my health and my fitness level for over a decade now. All because I resolved conscious and Shadow issues and took guidance from Higher Self. I came to realize that my health is for me, not for anyone else. I became pono with myself and what I need to do for my health.

A few studies point to this same concept. One, published in the New England Journal of Medicine, found that people who quit smoking for themselves and not for others have a higher success rate. I've had people say to me, "But isn't it admirable, the person who quit smoking for their kids because they want to live longer?" Admirable, maybe, but they have a lower success rate. The ego alone has a hard time being effective at anything, much less major change. It takes the cooperation of the Higher Self and subconscious to do it. A healthy ego knows this. A healthy ego is the individual who knows the foundation, knows the path.

My teacher Etua has three guidelines: Know where you've come from, what you are doing now, and know who you are.

EGO & SUBCONSCIOUS

An unhealthy ego is disconnected from the subconscious and the wisdom of the subconscious, and therefore it gets in the way of resolving things like the Shadow (that part of the subconscious that holds and often hides aspects of ourselves that we consider negative). I won't discuss the subconscious in depth here but most of us have at least an inkling of what the subconscious is. And when the conscious mind refuses to listen to the subconscious, it can create massive problems.

An example is the father who comes home after a bad day at work. Not knowing how to resolve his emotions, yells at his kids because a short fuse is in place. The kids don't understand: "Dad, why are you yelling at us? We're just playing." Rather than recognizing and owning up to the fact that he has some issues to deal with, the dad justifies his actions. "This is for your own good." But a healthy ego that stays connected to the subconscious will understand what's going on. "You know what, kids? I apologize. I had a stressful day. Please forgive me. I need some quiet time to work it out." No excuses, no "I have to be the king, I have to be in control all the time." When the ego connects to the subconscious, it realizes that negative emotions are a clue to some type of learning. The balanced ego uses this information rather than suppressing it.

The ego casts a shadow. The ego casts a shadow just like your physical body casts a shadow when the light of the sun illuminates it. It is the bright light of the Self or Higher Consciousness, your Self's illumination, that casts a shadow when it hits the ego. Jung believed that knowing this Shadow and the ego that casts it are critical to realizing who you truly are and your foundation. Isn't that the purpose of any spiritual study, to know who and what you are and what your foundation is? The ego is responsible for directing this exploration of all parts of you. It is the ego that drives you forward to know your foundation, know what your limits are, know where your strengths are, know when you need help or change.

But an unhealthy ego gets in the way of allowing the unconscious, that emotional side of who you are, to have a say in things that you do or decisions you make. Trusting your intuition and your visceral gut feelings is the sign of a healthy ego, a statement that you know who you are.

John Ka'imikaua taught that in ancient times in Hawai'i, people who trusted their na'au (their gut, core or center) and their instinct were considered to be the more intelligent than those who relied on the analytical conscious mind. I think in modern times it shouldn't be conscious mind overruling the unconscious / na'au or the na'au overruling the conscious mind. It should be an integration of both, incorporating the Higher Conscious mind as well, so that decisions are pono on all levels. We live in a world that teaches our conscious minds far beyond what we ever have had before. There are times that you do need to think things through, analyze the data, and weigh all factors. There are other times when you do need to say, "Look, I may not be able to explain it fully but I know who I am and I know what I know."

1. Are there areas in your life where you consciously desire to make changes but can't bring yourself to make them? Where willpower just hasn't been enough?

2. Have you felt a call toward a different life but... a) it doesn't make sense? b) it isn't that clear? c) you have no idea how to get there? d) it feels like this call maybe reached the wrong number?

BACK TO THE BEGINNING AGAIN

I've taken you through a lot of concepts. But the idea is that you end up with working concepts so you can effectively use we've all been born with: conscious mind, unconscious mind and higher self. It's like we've all got this high-powered equipment, with technological capabilities that can do anything we want! But where's the operating manual?

Getting my PhD in Health Psychology, I had to study a bunch of "operating manuals" – various disciplines in psychology. They all shared a lot of the same basics. But their take on those basics was very different. In all my studies, I feel most connected to the operating manuals of Carl Jung and Huna. These two have made the most sense to me and have benefited me personally the most.

I've focused on the conscious mind in this first book. The conscious mind (ego and persona) has gotten a bad rap in spiritual circles. Some spiritual paths say to "kill it" or "kill the ego!" But from the previous chapters, you now know that the conscious mind has a really important role to play as:

- The orchestra conductor bringing all the parts together.

- The goal setter determining where this ship is headed.

- The good facilitator/listener who can pay attention to messages from the unconscious and higher self.

In the West and in Western ways of approaching life, maybe the conscious mind has become too prominent. It's as if we're supposed to only live life by our conscious, analytical intelligence. But from previous chapters you now know that your conscious mind:

- Makes better decisions when it coordinates with unconscious and higher self.

- Can choose to change – but can only make change happen by engaging the unconscious and higher self.

- Can only access the experience of higher self (God) through the unconscious.

So you have a good understanding of the conscious mind's function, what it is and what it isn't. It's not all of who you are but it's got an important role to play. Conscious mind deserves our respect.

Epilogue

In the next book, I'll spend a fair amount of time talking about what Jung referred to as the Shadow. The Shadow is a pretty potent force whose power can be negative or positive, depending on your relationship to it. Not an aspect of yourself you want to ignore! What are the Shadow elements you are projecting into your life? I'll then cover the opposites, what they mean, how you reconcile and balance them. Jung referred to opposites as anima, animus. Huna refers to them as [dichotomy], masculine, feminine. In addition to that discussion, we'll look at some of the other major aspects that are part of the Jungian approach, for example, what Jung referred to as the hero, or the hero's journey. I'll also spend time looking at mother and father and the roles they play.

In the last book, I'll define what it means to connect with the Self. Once you've reconciled Shadow and the opposites, the next focus is on connection with the Self with a capital S. If he had lived in a different day and age, I think Jung would have easily referred to Self as "Higher Self." Huna delves into Higher Self in detail, and we'll cover the prime directives of the Higher Self in depth from the Huna perspective.

The last book of the series will also cover another way of looking at the three energies of being, doing, and having, and life's constant cycle. Life is an aim. It's not an end, which means that once you get to a certain level and you say, "Aha, I have self realized. I have my purpose," you get to start again. You get to take it up to another level, then take it up to another level and another.

About the Author

Matthew B. James, MA, PhD

Matthew B. James, MA, Ph.D., is President of Kona University which offers integrative psychology and clinical therapeutic degrees; and President of The Empowerment Partnership, where he serves as a master trainer of Neuro Linguistic Programming (NLP), a practical behavioral technology for helping people achieve their desired results in life. Dr. James delivers seminars and cultural trainings throughout the United States, Canada, Asia, and Europe. Due to his expertise on post-traumatic stress disorder (PTSD), indigenous cultures and his research on forgiveness, Dr. James is a regular Psychology Today blog contributor and is often quoted in magazines, newspapers and has been featured on Fox News, CNN Headline News and many other TV and radio shows around the world.

As an international speaker and educator, he embodies the principles he teaches. His first book, The Foundation of Huna: Ancient Wisdom for Modern Times, details forgiveness and meditation techniques used in Hawaii for hundreds of years. Dr. James carries on the lineage of one of the last practicing kahuna of mental health and well-being. These traditions span 28 generations and have been presented to the United Nations to further peace amongst diverse countries and cultures.

The focus of Dr. James' educational commitments include stress reduction, trust between practitioner and client, as well as rapport building to improve efficacy and results in the healing arts. Furthermore, Dr. James focuses on leadership models to improve communication within families, organizations and communities.

Dr. James' degrees include a Ph.D. in Health (Integrative) Psychology from Walden University. His residency was at Indiana University. His dissertation was titled "Ho'oponopono: Assessing the Effects of a Traditional Hawaiian Forgiveness Technique on Unforgiveness," and is available in print, or online through UMI or ProQuest.

www.nlp.com

www.huna.com

27428385R00074

Printed in Great Britain
by Amazon